German Military Combat Dress

1939-1945

Chris Ellis

ALMARK PUBLISHING CO. LTD., LONDON

First published—April 1973

ISBN 0 85524 116 0 (hard cover edition)
ISBN 0 85524 117 9 (paper covered edition)

Printed in Great Britain by
Vale Press Ltd., Mitcham, Surrey CR4 4HR
for the publishers, Almark Publishing Co. Ltd.,
270 Burlington Road, New Malden,
Surrey KT3 4NL, England.

Introduction

THIS book is the successor to one of the earlier and most popular Almark books *German Combat Uniforms, 1939-1945.*

The latter book sold well over 20,000 copies in two years and after six printings the blocks were inevitably showing signs of wear. Rather than simply replace the original blocks, we have taken the opportunity of revising the basic format completely, utilising some drawings, diagrams and pictures from *German Combat Uniforms,* but adding very many new ones. The text is completely new and the contents are arranged in a rather more logical order than before. The new title, aside from being slightly more explicit, serves to distinguish this new book from the old.

It must be emphasised that this volume retains the original object, namely to serve as a basic concise guide to German Army, Waffen-SS and Luftwaffe combat dress in an inexpensive form. There are now a number of more specialist volumes covering uniforms of individual arms and branches and some of these are listed in the appendix.

This book aims to give a broad overall coverage sufficient to furnish the wargamer, model soldier collector, uniform enthusiast and any interested layman with a working knowledge of the subject. The dress variations in the Wehrmacht were many and complicated, and it would not be possible to include every single item in a small volume like this. The emphasis here is on the dress worn on active service, and parade dress and similar orders are not covered. The colour pictures in this edition are from wartime German sources. Some of the line illustrations, especially of badges and ranks are taken from wartime intelligence publications. Small arms and the more common infantry weapons are included in this book, again in brief detail to assist in indentifying the types of weapon more commonly seen in photographs of the period.

Author and publisher wish to thank the following for assistance with information, photographs and other material used in this book, (and it predecessor); Peter Chamberlain, Brian L. Davis, Gerhard Elser, D. S. V. Fosten, S. R. Gordon-Douglas, David List, R. Marrion, Fred Vos, P. J. Atkinson, and J. Lucas. Picture sources include the Imperial War Museum and German wartime publications. Some of the drawings are from U.S. Army recognition material and several new illustrations for this volume, in colour and line, have been drawn by Alan Kemp.

CONTENTS

An MG 34 team of an assault engineer battalion ferrying across a river during the invasion of France in May 1940. The team commander, an unteroffizier, sits in the bow. Note the supports for the belt on the greatcoat of the centre man. The assault boat steersman (right) carries goggles for protection from spray (IWM-MH9417).

FRONT COVER: MG 34 team in Norway, April 1940. The team commander, an unteroffitzier, is on the right, wearing field grey wool gloves. Web bands are fitted to the helmets for the attachment of foliage; in this case, however, whitewash has been preferred due to the wintery local conditions.

BACK COVER: Assault engineers spearheaded major attacks and this team in France, May 1940, carries typical equipment including smoke flares, wire cutters, stick grenades, and demolition charges. Their task was to break through enemy defence systems for the main infantry force. The men are wearing the standard 1936 pattern service dress and all carry Luger ·08 pistols (IWM-MH9231).

OPPOSITE: An artillery observer—an unteroffizier (left)—passing ranges to his gefreiter assistant during the campaign in France, May 1940. The men are wearing typical smart well cared for uniform of the period. Note the gas cape (gasplane) case slung on the chest of the gefreiter. This was not usually carried later in the war (IWM-MH9199).

1: The Army (Heer)

GERMAN serivce and combat dress garments in the World War 2 period were characterised by a balanced combination of functional design and a smart appearance and finish. The quality was excellent, though from 1942 onwards as drastic economies were made, there was a marked falling off in standard. It must be emphasised that exceptions to the rule were legion and many typical exceptions are illustrated. The text which follows is for clarity broken down into sections with each type of dress covered in turn.

1936 PATTERN SERVICE DRESS

The basic Army service dress on issue at the start of World War 2 had been introduced in 1936 to replace the old Wiemarian uniforms. The tunic (feldbluse) was of field grey wool material with a turn down collar. The front buttoned to the neck and had five field grey painted metal buttons. There were four pleated patch pockets each with a pointed flap secured by a field grey painted button. The tunic had four metal supports in which the waist belt fitted. For parades and formal occasions the tunic was buttoned to the neck, but on campaign it

LEFT: Sentry in Norway, April 1940, showing the normal guard or drill order with the waistbelt and ammunition pouches only. Note the dark green facing on shoulder straps and collar.

RIGHT: Signal dog team in France, 1940. The Waffenfarbe (coloured piping) denoting the branch (probably yellow—signals) is clearly visible on the shoulder straps of the nearest man. This picture, and that on the left, shows the two sides of the helmet with the national shield (right side) and eagle emblem (left side) in decal form (IWM-MH1907).

RIGHT: Normal service and walking out dress consisted of the basic uniform, waistbelt, and feldmütze forage cap. This man is on cook-house duty, collecting hot box meals for a gun crew on the French coast, 1942.

could be worn open at the neck for comfort. The collar was faced in a very dark bottle green material. There were detachable shoulder straps also faced in the dark bottle green material. Prior to 1938 the shoulder straps were pointed at their inner ends for enlisted men, but thereafter a rounded end was adopted.

The early pattern shoulder strap was still in wear by some units or individuals well into the war period. Shoulder straps are illustrated and described in more detail later. Officer's tunics were nominally of the same pattern as the enlisted men. Many officers in the field wore enlisted men's tunics, but it was usual to wear a privately made tunic of better quality material with pockets of rather neater cut. The cuffs on this tunic were of the turn-back variety, while the enlisted men's pattern tunic had plain cuffs. Senior NCOs also sometimes wore officer's quality tunics.

The trousers worn with service dress were of the same wool field grey material as the tunic. They had side slit pockets, a fly front and a high waist—suspenders (braces) held the trousers up but there was a small buckle strap at the rear to tighten the fit at the waist.

Because these service dress garments faded slightly with age, (and cleaning), there was sometimes some slight discrepancy in shade between tunic and trousers. Mounted troops, drivers and officers wore field grey wool breeches as an alternative to trousers depending on duty requirements. Breeches were the more usual wear for officers on staff and administrative duties, and often in the field too.

Beneath the tunic was worn a shirt, either plain grey wool or field

ABOVE: The service trousers had a small adjusting buckle strap at rear and were cut high at the waist. The loose fitting light grey service shirt is also shown. In the centre of this group is the units' senior NCO wearing a service cap and a double band of silver lace on his cuff to denote his position as 'Der Spiess'—sergeant-major. Man on right is wearing drill trousers, nominally white but here extremely dirty.

grey cotton material, the latter with breast pockets and atachments for shoulder straps when the tunic was not worn. A cloth neck band was provided for wear when the collar was buttoned up. In practice what was worn under the tunic depended on circumstances. For example, in cold weather a wool jersey might be favoured. Sometimes, on campaign, a non regulation neck scarf was worn with the tunic collar open.

Officers wore brown leather belts and, until 1939, a brown 'Sam Browne' cross-belt. Enlisted ranks wore a black leather belt which also formed part of the personal equipment on field service. Officers' belts had a plain metal buckle while enlisted men's belts had a white metal plate type buckle with a 'Gott Mit Uns' (God With Us), inscription, on a circular device featuring the national eagle emblem.

On some formal occasions in the 1939-40 period it was possible to see units parading in the field grey service tunic worn with grey parade dress trousers, but parade dress as such was not issued after the outbreak of war and is beyond the scope of this book.

A greatcoat was issued for wear over service dress, this being made of field grey wool material with a deep fold down collar, which could be turned up and buttoned with a flap at the front for cold weather wear. The collar was faced with dark bottle green material and shoulder straps were worn appropriate to rank and status. The greatcoat was nominally the same pattern for all ranks. It had deep turn-back cuffs, a half-belt and two buttons at the back and full pleated skirts reaching below the knee. On parade and formal occasions the service belt was worn outside the greatcoat. On campaign the men's personal equipment was also worn outside the greatcoat. Officers could be

RIGHT: The pattern of white metal buckle for the enlisted man's waistbelt. Officers had a plain buckle of the conventional frame and bar type.

seen wearing issue greatcoats, but usually they had them in a superior quality material made privately by military tailors as with their uniforms. Officers of general rank also had the standard pattern greatcoat, but it had gilt butons and the inside of the front flaps had bright red facings. The top two buttons were left undone and the lapels showed the red facing to the front.

As an alternative to a greatcoat, officers often wore a field grey leather overcoat which was supplied by military tailors. This was cut

Victory in the West; a rifle section (squad) of a motorised infantry unit moves up through a Belgian village street during the invasion of France and Flanders in May 1940. Note the grenades and gas sheet (gasplane) cases. The goggles were worn when riding in the half-track carrier or truck. This unit still wears its regimental number on the shoulder strap though this practice was later discarded for security reasons (IWM).

ABOVE AND BELOW: Infantry in Norway, April 1940, show the greatcoat worn in combat conditions. The full personal equipment could in theory be worn over the greatcoat but this was awkward and most men resorted to the waistbelt only with as much equipment as possible suspended from it, the braces being omitted. See page 4, in contrast, for a view of the braces in wear with the greatcoat. RIGHT: The superior cut and quality of the officer's greatcoat is immediately obvious. General Von Brauchitsch is here observing operations on the Eastern Front in 1941. Second from right is an ADC wearing silver cord aiguillettes to denote his status as a staff officer. Far right is a mountain troops officer in jackboots, and near left are officers in grey leather greatcoats. The officer's waistbelt buckle is also well shown here.

in similar style to the greatcoat, but there were variations in detail. Shoulder straps were supposed to be worn with this coat but were sometimes omitted.

FOOTWEAR

With the 1936 pattern uniform the normal service wear was originally knee length black leather boots—known commonly as 'jackboots'. Officers in breeches wore black leather riding boots or jackboots. Senior officers almost invariably wore the former. Also issued were black leather lace up ankle boots. These were worn when walking out, (or in other orders of dress). Some mounted troops wore the ankle boots with breeches and field grey cloth wrap-around puttees in place of riding boots.

As the war progressed leather became scarce and from 1942 onwards the ankle boot became common wear with canvas gaiters secured with leather straps. These anklet-type gaiters were very similar to the contemporary British pattern. Even before 1942 however, the ankle boot and anklets had been worn by some units in the field.

Pictorial evidence shows some troops on the Russian Front wearing blankets as early as winter 1941-42.

RIGHT: In summer the sleeves of the tunic were often rolled up. On the march the men often went bareheaded. Note the various ways of wearing the equipment. Man on left wears gaiters and ankle boots. Nearest man carries a leather map case on the left side of his belt. These are infantrymen with an 'acquired' horse. BELOW: General-Leutnant von Manteuffel (left), his ADC (centre) and Major Kriegk, commander of Pz.Gr.Rgt. 'Grossdeutschland'. Both the general and his ADC are wearing the pre-1942 type officers' field service cap with soft crown and no cords. The general's cap was, however, piped in gold. Major Kriegk is wearing the lightweight drill feldmütze as originally issued to the Afrika Korps. The Waffenfarbe strips in the major's collar patch can be clearly seen.

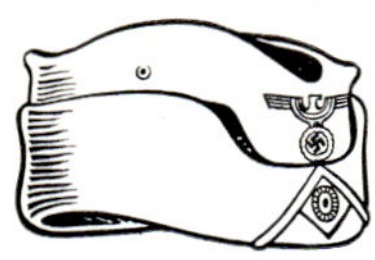
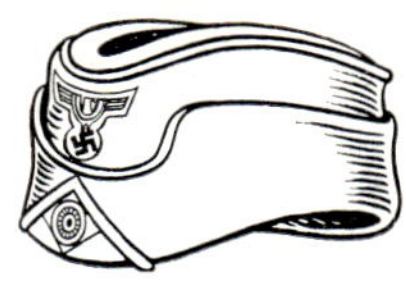

ABOVE: The Army pattern M1938 feldmütze, enlisted men's pattern on left and officers pattern (with silver piping on crown) on right. Chevron was in arm-of-service colour (US Official). RIGHT: The later M1942 feldmütze had a plainer front with no chevron and two buttons. to facilitate wear with the flaps turned down and buttoned under the chin in cold weather.

HEADWEAR

All ranks were issued with a service cap which had a black patent leather peak and was field grey with a dark bottle green hat band. The crown was stiffened by a wire loop, but (especially on campaign), this was often removed to give the crown a 'sloppy' shapeless look. The cap was piped in arm of service colours except for generals, when the piping was gold. Enlisted men's caps had a leather front-strap, but officers' caps had silver cords and side buttons.

A cockade in national colours (red/white/black) with metal oak leaf surround and the national (eagle) emblem, decorated the cap front. For generals the cap cords were in gold lace, as was the oak leaf surround from 1943. The service cap was normally worn for parades and formal occasions by enlisted men. In the field it was worn only by officers, staff, some NCOs and special duty men.

For fatigues' drill, and campaign wear, the field service cap (feldmütze) was universal. This was a 'garrison' style field grey fore-and-aft cap which was designed to be worn under the helmet if required. The sides of the cap were designed to fold down and so cover the back of the neck in very cold weather. The feldmütze (1938 pattern) was decorated at the front with the national emblems, plus an inverted chevron which indicated the arm of service by its colour. In 1942 a simpler pattern feldmütze was introduced which had its side flaps secured by two front buttons, displacing the front chevron decoration. The officers' feldmütze was in superior quality material and had silver piping (gold for generals) on the crown. Before 1942, officers' also wore a simplified form of the service cap (no cap cords, inferior quality badges and no stiffeners) as a field service cap.

In 1943, a new peaked field cap, the einheitsfeldmütze, was introduced for all ranks. With a long soft peak, simplified national badge, and piping as before it became almost universal wear. The einheitsfeldmütze was derived from earlier types of cap used by mountain troops and the Afrika Korps (described later).

The steel helmet was the distinctive 'coal scuttle' type which characterised German military dress. Prior to 1936 and for some years afterwards the 1916 pattern steel helmet was on issue. This was large and deep complete with two prominent lugs which were

ABOVE: An infantryman resting, with his equipment laid out to show anti-gas respirator case, Kar 98K rifle, greatcoat, zeltbahn, helmet, and, in this instance, a leather map case.

originally intended to hold a face visor. In 1935 a new pattern helmet was produced without the lugs and with a more streamlined shape. The 1935 pattern helmet was later supplemented by a 1943 pattern helmet of simpler construction but similar shape. In practice, all these helmts could be seen in use in the World War 2 period at the appropriate periods. The 1916 pattern helmet was worn mainly by reserve and second line units from 1939. Helmets were painted field grey and originally carried decals on each side portraying the

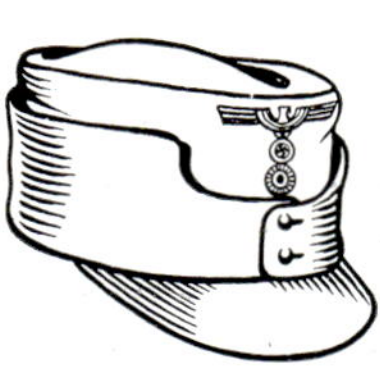

LEFT: The M1943 Einheitsfeldmütze shown with flaps down in cold weather, in normal wear, and in closer detail. Later the badges shown were of a cheaper type on a triangular cloth background (US Official).

national emblem and national colours. These decals depicted a red/white/black shield on the right and a national eagle in 'Brandenburg' style on the left side. In late 1940 these markings were discontinued though helmets so marked were still seen in use for some time afterwards.

1943 PATTERN SERVICE DRESS

As the war lengthened and Germany's resources were stretched, numerous economies were effected. In the case of uniforms a major change was the simplification of service dress garments. The feldbluse was changed to have slightly shorter skirts and plain pockets with shorter straight-edged flaps. All the dark green facing material was

TOP OF PAGE: Infantry on the march in 1940, disembarking in Norway, carrying their large pack and all equipment in full marching order. Note MG 34 teams carrying ammunition boxes and the helmets slung from waistbelt. LEFT: MG 34 team in Russia, 1943. Note the plain collars and shoulder straps typical of this late period. The helmet is the 1935 model worn with leather straps for the attachment of local foliage when under cover.

This June 1940 picture shows well the 1935 pattern steel helmet with and without decals, the standard leather pistol holster on the gefreiter's waistbelt, the cuff slits, and the prominent seams on the service tunic. Captured French soldier is in centre.

omitted from the collar and shoulder straps, though a few early 1943 pattern tunics retained this feature.

Concurrently the 1936 pattern tunic remained on issue while stocks lasted (or old garments were refurbished) and this pattern tunic was also to be seen without the bottle green facings. Trousers were also simplified with the introduction of the self supporting type with attached belt.

All the 1943 pattern clothing was of inferior quality material with the wool content greatly reduced and replaced with artificial fibres. The resulting garments were less hard wearing than the earlier patterns, and looked rather less smart.

This also applied to the greatcoat which lost its facing material from the collar and shoulder straps, and became less elegant in shape owing to the inferior material. A 1943 pattern greatcoat was issued which was of much inferior quality and had a distinctive deep collar which could be turned up to afford maximum protection in inclement weather. Variations on this basic coat existed including a type with extra upper side pockets and added lining especially for winter combat wear.

ABOVE: A general in service dress and greatcoat, showing the red facing on the collar. INSET, ABOVE: Detail of general's collar patch. ABOVE, RIGHT: Officer of Panzerjäger (tank destroyer) troops in the special field grey AFV uniform and 1943 pattern Einheitsfeldmütze. Note Panzer pink Waffenfarbe and ribbon of Iron Cross 2nd Class. RIGHT: Panzer-Grenadier in 1942. He has both rifle and Schmeisser ammunition pouches, helmet cover, canvas gaiters and carries a slung MP38. INSET, RIGHT: Shoulder strap of Oberleutnant showing pink Panzer Waffenfarbe and regimental number—discarded in 1939.

ABOVE: German prisoners in Russia, early 1944, showing clearly the contrast between the 1943 pattern tunic (plain collar and shoulder straps, no pocket pleats) with the earlier tunic worn by the man second from left. Man on extreme left wears a standard issue face net which was used mainly on the Russian front for insect protection (in swampy areas) but had secondary camouflage value. BELOW: Infantry in Russia, summer 1943 showing the 1943 pattern tunic, gaiters, and Einheitsfeld-mütze in wear.

TOP: An infantry platoon on the march, 1944, each rifle squad being led by its unteroffizier. The unteroffizier in the centre wears the more abbreviated 1943 pattern tunic, the others wearing the 1936 pattern garment. Note the Einheitsfeldmütze carried tucked in the men's belts. Platoon officer is just visible on horseback in the background. ABOVE: Presentation of Iron Crosses to NCOs (first two on right) and an officer. Back to camera is the general's ADC wearing staff officer's aiguillettes.

1944 PATTERN SERVICE DRESS

To effect further economies, a new type of service dress, based closely on British battledress, was introduced in 1944. This was a field grey material in blouse form with waist-band. It had non-pleated pockets at the front and a six-button front. The later self-supporting trousers were used with this pattern uniform and ankle boots and gaiters were invariably worn. Badges and insignia were of a simplified

ABOVE: The '08 pattern machine gun was still in wide front line use in the early part of the war. This team in Norway, 1940, are using the weapon in the AA role. They wear the 1935 pattern helmet and the standard pattern great-coat. They also wear field grey wool scarves, another standard cold weather garment. LEFT: This unteroffizier (sergeant) in France, May 1940, wears standard service dress with the 1936 pattern tunic and 1938 pattern feldmütze. Of special interest is the pre-1939 pattern shoulder strap which had a pointed, rather than a rounded end.

ABOVE: A feldwebel of Panzer troops in early 1940. He wears the special black AFV suit (same pattern as the field grey suit shown on page 17) with the schutzmütze AFV cap which incorporated a protective leather helmet beneath the beret. Note pink Waffenfarbe and Iron Cross 2nd Class ribbon. BELOW: Mountain troops assembling a 7·5 cm pack gun. Note Edelweiss badges on cap and sleeve.

ABOVE, LEFT: The 1944 pattern service dress, based on British battle dress in style. Note eagle emblem on breast cheaply made on cloth patch. ABOVE, RIGHT: Gebirgsjäger (mountain troops) in service dress wearing Army pattern camouflage smock, white side out. This was mainly worn by infantry, but was also worn by some mountain troops late in the war as an alternative to the anoraks shown on page 26.

and inferior type. The 1944 pattern issue was still not widespread when the war ended.

MOUNTAIN TROOPS

Mountain troops wore a version of the standard service dress adapted for their special duties. The feldbluse was the service type (and carried the distinctive mountain troops' Edelweiss sleeve badge) but the trousers were gathered in at the ankle and worn with high cut mountain climbing boots. Some variations to this were common, especially in the 1939-40 period. Officers, in particular, often favoured wrap around field grey cloth puttees or civilian style spats. Tyrolean type wool stockings, reaching nearly to the knee outside climbing breeches were in fact the pre-war style for mountain troops, and they continued in wear with some units in the early part of the war. Staff

Mountain troops in standard service dress, showing Bergemütze cap and cloth puttees. Mule handlers slung rifles to front as shown. This is a 7·5 cm mountain gun detachment in training.

Mountain troops' specialised clothing. LEFT TO RIGHT: The sage green wind jacket worn with ski trousers, puttees, and climbing boots. Heavy sheepskin coat, fur winter cap with toques, and felt and leather winter boots—issued to all fighting arms for special duties (eg, sentries). Service dress with puttees and climbing boots. SS-VT gebirgsjäger in pre-1939 pattern field grey service dress, here with tunic worn open at neck. Luftwaffe NCO attached to mountain unit, wearing Luftwaffe service dress with mountain pattern cap, puttees, and climbing boots (U.S. Official).

ABOVE: Men of a motor-cycle reconnaissance company resting. The driver is wearing the standard grey waterproof coat issued to all motor-cyclists. Note the plain collar and shoulder straps on the 1936 pattern tunic. BELOW: MG34 team of the SS-Polizei Division, a Waffen-SS formation made up of policemen conscripted for military service. They wear the Waffen-SS arm eagle but the police escutcheon in place of the national emblem on the helmet, May 1940.

ABOVE: General Rommel (left) with senior officers in the Western Desert, about June 1941. All wear the reed green tropical uniform with shorts except the officer extreme right who is in breeches. BELOW: MG34 team on watch in the desert, about August 1942 shows how the tropical uniform washed out and faded to a sandy colour. Loader wears normal 1938 pattern feldmütze. Note different shades of individual garments.

ABOVE: Mountain troops wear the special reversible anorak, white side out. It was field grey the other side for wear below the snow line. Note fitted hood and drawstring neck.

ABOVE: Sage green wind jacket was issued to about 10% of mountain troops. It was loose fitting and rank was denoted by shoulder straps. RIGHT: 1943 pattern windproof suit for mountain troops, was reversible —white one side and tan the other.

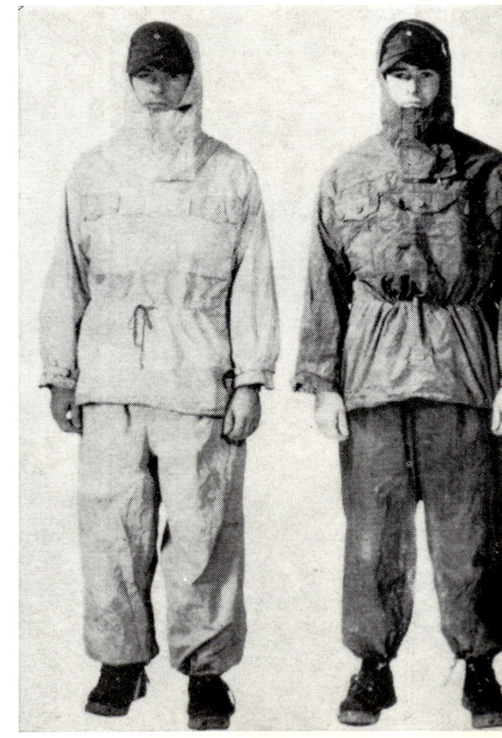

The commander of 3rd Mountain Division (centre) with his staff in 1940. The various styles of breeches, puttees, and gaiters were particularly characteristic of the early war period. Short cloth puttees at ankle level were usual wear as shown on page 23 (IWM-GER1265).

officers could be seen in breeches and riding boots as a further variation in dress. The headwear for mountain troops was a distinctive, peaked, forage cap (Gebirgsmütze); this carried an Edelweiss badge on the left side. The Gebirgsmütze formed a pattern which was closely copied for the Einheitsmütze generally issued in 1943. The steel helmet was, of course, also issued to mountain troops. A distinctive garment for mountain troops in the early part of the war was a sage green waterproof wind jacket, double breasted and reaching to the thighs. This coat was issued to only about 10% of the men and it was supplemented by a windproof anorak with drawstring neck and two breast pockets. The anorak was reversible, field grey one side and white the other. It had an attached hood. In 1943 a new pattern windproof rayon suit was issued, consisting of a reversible anorak and trouser coveralls in the same proofed material. Both garments were white one side and tan coloured the other side. The anorak had a hood, a drawstring waist and three pockets (each side) across the chest. In addition to these specialised garments, mountain troops also wore the standard reversible camouflage smock (described later) shown on page 22. Ski trousers and ski boots were worn in appropriate circumstances and were issued to all mountain troops.

ARMOUR (PANZER) TROOPS

For duty in tanks and armoured cars, a special black service uniform was issued. This consisted of a short double breasted tunic (or blouse) and trousers gathered in at the ankle and which were worn with leather ankle boots. The tunic had a turned down collar and deep revers which were opened to reveal a grey shirt and a collar with a

ABOVE: Two views of the special two piece reversible winter suit, issued on the Russian front. The white side is shown but on extreme right the trousers are being worn field grey side outwards, and field grey is visible inside the hood. Skier on left is wearing his feldmütze cap with wool toques to keep his head warm. BELOW: Metal cap badges for Mountain troops (left) and Jäger troops (right), worn on left side of cap. Jäger badge was issued from 1942. BOTTOM: Sleeve badges for Mountain troops (left)—white and yellow—and Jäger troops —light green—worn on right sleeve.

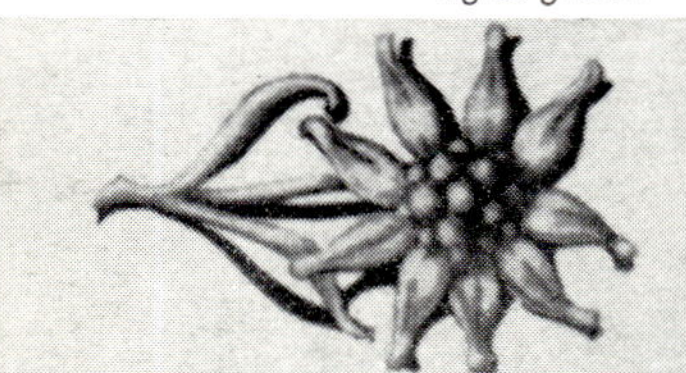

ABOVE: Troopers of the Waffen-SS 'Florian Geyer' Cavalry Division, Russian Front, 1942. Cavalry wore breeches instead of trousers. The Waffen-SS reversible smock is shown with the predominantly green 'summer' pattern mottle camouflage. A browner 'winter' pattern was on the inside. BELOW: Assault troops cross a river in Russia 1942. Note how well the helmet camouflage merges with the adjacent reeds. Shoulder straps and collars are in plain field grey.

An officer of Panzer troops briefing tank crews in early 1940 before the invasion of France. He is wearing the early type of officer's field cap, a simpler version of the service cap, devoid of straps and lace. The men wear the schutzmütze and all are in the blank panzer suits (IWM-HU1206).

black wool tie. The tunic front could be buttoned up to the neck, however, if required. Distinctive 'Death's Head' (skull) devices in white metal were worn within piped patches on the collar and shoulder straps displayed rank badges in the conventional way. The edge of the collar and turn backs were piped in the arm of service colour (Waffenfarbe), in this case, Rose Pink. The amount of piping on the uniform was drastically reduced in 1942. An exception to the rule was 24.Pz.Rgt., formerly the 1st Cavalry Regiment, who retained the yellow Waffenfarbe of the cavalry.

A special form of headwear was designed, protective in nature, for AFV troops. This was the Schutzmütze, a floppy black beret, worn over a leather dome-like crash helmet. The beret carried the national cockade plus a wreath of oak leaves in silver lace. This particular form of headwear was discontinued early in 1940 and was replaced with a black form of the feldmütze forage cap. In turn, this was replaced in 1943 with a black version of the einheitsfeldmütze. Badges, belt, etc on the panzer uniform, corresponded to those on the ordinary service dress—except where noted above.

In 1940 when the first assault guns were put into service, a new uniform was designed for assault gun crews. This was a field grey version of the panzer crew suit described above. It was similar in all respects except that the Schutzmütze helmet was not worn at any time—it had been discontinued before the first assault guns entered service. Any appropriate headgear—helmet, service cap, feldmütze, etc—could be seen worn with these special AFV uniforms.

RIGHT: An assault gun crewman with his short jacket removed to show suspenders (braces), grey shirt and tie. Trousers for AFV personnel were always gathered into ankle boots. BELOW: The field grey AFV suit being worn by officers of an assault gun unit in the 'Grossdeutschland' Division. This élite division was one of the few Army formations to wear a cuff title (left). Officer at right wears his service cap—with lace and strap, etc. Compare with field cap shown opposite. Note that the regiment's commanding officer (centre) is wearing ordinary service dress with feldmütze cap, and breeches.

TROPICAL AND HOT WEATHER DRESS

Tropical clothing first made its appearance early in 1941 when the advance units of what became the Afrika Korps arrived in Libya. As originally issued the uniform included a light weight heavy linen (denim) tunic, similar in cut to the ordinary service dress tunic, except that the collar was open in style with fashioned revers. Long trousers (and breeches for officers) in the same material were supplied, and

ABOVE, LEFT: Flieger (private) of Luftwaffe Flak troops, 1940, wearing service dress. The shirt and tie were worn on formal occasions or on duty. In combat enlisted men did not normally wear them. This man carries a unit number on his shoulder strap, a practice which was discontinued early in the war. ABOVE, RIGHT: Unterfeldwebel (staff sergeant) of Fallschirmjäger, 1940, wearing Fliegerbluse beneath smock. Gloves were worn when jumping. INSET, TOP: Detail of collar patch of Fallschirmjäger Unterfeldwebel. INSET, CENTRE: Early (1939-40) wound badge, worn on left breast. INSET, ABOVE: Luftwaffe pattern of national emblem. INSET, LEFT: Specialist badge for Luftwaffe Flak personnel—worn on left cuff.

Newly arrived members of what soon was to become the Afrika Korps, parading in Tripoli in April 1941. They are wearing freshly issued reed green tropical uniforms, with canvas and leather boots, and tropical helmets. Note similarity of uniform style to normal field grey service dress.

these were worn with high front-laced boots (almost knee height) made of leather and green canvas. A matching drill shirt and tie were worn —allowing the jacket to be removed if required—and a tropical pith helmet, canvas covered, was provided for headwear. The standard national and army emblems were worn on metal shields each side of the helmet, matching the postioning of these markings on the steel helmet. A lightweight forage cap, similar in style to the peaked gebirgsmütze, but without folding sides, was also issued.

Numerous individual changes and variations followed. An early disappearance was the cumbersome tropical helmet. Though some lingered on in use for the rest of the Africa campaign, most were discarded by late 1941 and the lightweight forage cap saw universal use. A lightweight version of the feldmütze was also produced, though not so widely worn as the cap. The high laced boots were also cumbersome and many men discarded them in favour of ordinary

ABOVE: Anti-tank gun crew in the Western Desert, May 1941. They are in the standard issue tropical suit but with the tunics discarded on this occasion. LEFT: A year later the formality of uniform in the desert had changed considerably. These men are in an assortment of styles, all based on the tropical dress but modified for comfort. Note the 'sand' painted helmet, and the varying degrees of fading in the different garments. Nearest man wears tropical leather and canvas boots cut down to ankle length.

ankle boots. Others cut the tops away from the tropical boots reducing them to ankle boot height. With these types of footwear the long trousers were worn with the bottoms gathered in at the ankle. Shorts were also issued—and sometimes long trousers were cut down to short length. With shorts in wear the legs were clad either in ankle socks and boots; long stockings and ankle boots; or stockings and/or the high laced tropical boots.

All the foregoing items of clothing were originally a light reed

Generals and senior officers in early 1943 when the forces in Tunis surrendered. Right and left of leading group are two Luftwaffe officers in tropical uniform. Of the two generals in front, one is wearing the regulation long canvas boots while the other wears his cut down to ankle length. All are wearing greatcoats. Note the 'Afrika Korps' cuff title on the first general's greatcoat (IWM-BNA2808).

green in colour (though batches of clothing were also issued in a light brown drill colour) but, under the influence of the desert sun and frequent washing, the original colouring soon disappeared and the clothing took on a 'neutral natural linen shade' with enormous variations in tone between individual garments.

There was also considerable variety in the method of wearing these clothes. As the campaign wore on, informal, comfortable, and other styles became the order of things. Non-standard jerseys and scarves were common, and regulations were not rigidly adhered to. The steel helmet when worn in the desert was painted sand-yellow, often with sand thrown over the wet paint to render the surface completely flat. Other helmet treatment usually consisted of a suitable cover—like a sandbag or white sheeting—stretched and stitched or pinned in place.

ABOVE: The standard tropical service uniform, here being worn by sentries in Crete. On the right is a senior Obergefreiter (over six years service) and on the left is a Leutnant. Note the piping on the officer's Einheitsmütze cap (IWM-JMH236).

RIGHT: A Generalmajor (Major General) of the Africa Korps in tropical uniform. He wears breeches and boots, service cap and full decorations on this occasion—surrender to the Allies in Tunis (IWM—BNA2895).

In the early part of 1943 the light reed green uniform was standardised for wear in summer conditions on all southern fronts, including Italy, the Balkans and the Crimea. Some units in Normandy and North West Europe in June 1944, were wearing this summer uniform too. In the more temperate zones, mixtures of dress could occur. For example, wool tunics with lightweight trousers depending on

A mixture of dress styles in Tunis, February 1943. General Von Armin (left) is wearing the rubberised motor-cyclist's waterproof coat, and goggles (obviously for travel in his staff car). The officer is in tropical dress and cap with a non-regulation scarf. The soldier wears a 'splinter' pattern Zeltbahn (poncho) over his tropical uniform.

circumstances. In the desert winter, too, there were additions like greatcoats, tunics, and extra jerseys to cope with extremes of temperature.

Introduced in 1943 was a light reed green denim two-piece tank suit, cut in the same style as the black and field grey versions and issued to tank and SP gun crews for summer wear.

For all these types of clothing the badge positions and styles were the same as for the normal service dress with the exceptions noted in the section on badges and insignia.

CAMOUFLAGE CLOTHING

The army did not issue camouflage clothing on such an extensive scale as the Waffen-SS (see later section). A standard camouflage garment, however, was the Zeltbahn, a camouflage quarter shelter, which was a poncho (cape) of triangular shape 8′ 3″ x 8′ 3″ x 6′ 3″ in

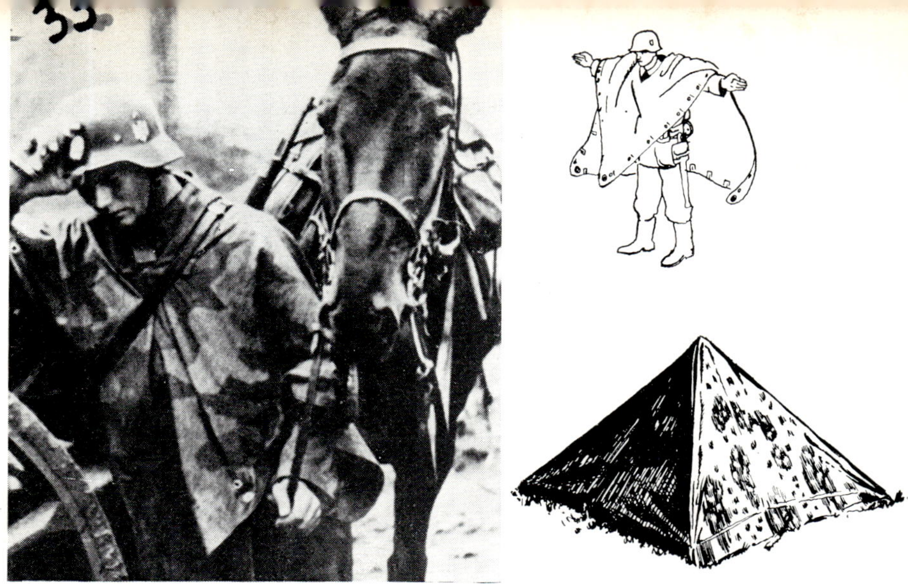

ABOVE, LEFT: Artilleryman wearing 'splinter' pattern Zeltbahn. ABOVE, RIGHT: Method of wearing Zeltbahn with (inset) the method of attaching four together to make a tent.

size. It was designed so that four Zeltbahns could be buttoned together to form a tent. A single Zeltbahn could provide a rudimentary bivouac for its owner, could be used as a groundsheet or could be worn as a cape by the owner inserting his head through a flapped slit in the middle. The hanging ends of the cape were then secured together. A motor cycle trooper could strap the ends round his legs and waist to prevent them fouling wheels, etc. A drawing shows the principle of this garment. When not in use it was folded up and secured within the owner's personal equipment. The Zeltbahn was made in proofed drill material and was finished off in a spring and summer camouflage (mainly green) on one side, and a winter and fall camouflage on the other (mainly brown).

The main Army camouflage style was the so-called 'splinter' pattern, made up mainly of jagged-edged long segments in various shades of green and brown. A lesser used alternative was a 'water' pattern where the segments of colour were run into each other producing a 'watery' effect as the colours merged into each other at the edges.

Camouflage helmet covers and smocks were introduced during 1942 and these were obviously inspired by the widespread issue of similar garments by the Waffen-SS. The standard camouflage patterns were used for the material; mainly 'splinter' type from pictorial evidence. The helmet cover was shaped to fit under the helmet rims and had loops of material attached to provide a hold for local foliage as a extra aid to concealment. The Army camouflage smock was cut full, had a lace-up neck, no collar, and cuffs. It had side slits for access to the tunic pockets underneath. The smock was reversible with 'splinter'

A late war picture of a MG42 team wearing the Army face mask (in 'water' pattern camouflage), 'splinter' pattern camouflaged forage caps, and 'water' pattern Army smocks. (see drawing of smock on page 22).

or 'water' pattern on the outside and was plain white inside for wear in the snow. The gebirgsjäger drawing on page 22 shows this garment in wear.

In the latter part of the war a camouflage suit was introduced, this being merely a camouflage printed version of the drill tropical suit with trousers and tunic, the latter with open turned down collar. This suit was not widely issued and it was possible to see the jacket only worn with field grey trousers and so on. 'Splinter' and 'water' pattern garments existed.

Various other camouflage items were used. Combat units in the field commonly utilised local foliage in their helmets to provide an added aid to concealment. A favourite method of holding the foliage

was by means of cycle tyre inner-tube strips round the helmet. Webbing straps were used for the same purpose. Net or sacking covers were alternatives for helmets. Several pictures in this book show typical styles adopted. A camouflage version of the einheitsfeldmütze saw limited issue, as did face masks for snipers and special troops. The face masks came in either camouflage or white material depending on season.

The most numerous variations in Army camouflage clothing were for winter wear. In the early part of the war—the first two winters—the snow camouflage dress was of an extemporised nature. White sheets fastened round the neck and/or helmet were the simplest form. There was also a white coverall which had sleeves and a hood to cover the helmet. This coverall was loose fitting, (for wear over equipment) and reached below the knees. A more abbreviated, shorter version of this garment, without the hood, was also produced. With this latter garment a separate white helmet cover was worn. In the latter part

The most basic snow camouflage garment was the coverall of white linen seen (right and opposite page) worn by Spanish volunteers of the famous 'Blue' division —a formation of Spanish troops under German Army command.

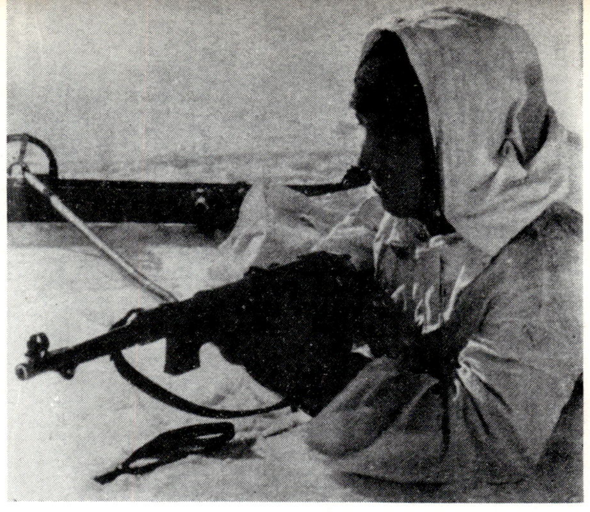

of the war more sophisticated snow camouflage garments were introduced. These included a two-piece overall suit—smock and trousers, the smock having a hood—and a one-piece overall suit worn like ordinary working overalls. This again had an attached hood for wear over the helmet. These garments were loose fitting so that extra layers of clothing or items of equipment could be worn underneath. All the foregoing garments were made in light cotton drill material and were purely for camouflage purposes.

After experiences in Russia in winter 1941-42, when conditions were severe, a special winter suit was quickly designed and manufactured for issue in the 1942-43 winter. This was a two-piece item consisting of trousers with webbing suspenders (braces) and a front-buttoning

The two-piece white winter suit (see also page 28) worn here by Panzer-Grenadiers following up an attack by Tiger tanks. Nearest man is wearing his trousers with the field grey outwards.

ABOVE, LEFT: In addition to field grey, the two-piece winter suit was also issued in 'splinter' or 'water' camouflage material, shown here worn on the outside. RIGHT: This stretcher bearer in Germany, 1945, appears to be wearing the white denim fatigue jacket as a form of snow camouflage. He wears a red cross armband and a red cross vest showing to front and rear. Note the gefreiter rank chevrons on the left sleeve. (IWM-BU2958).

smock. Two layers of windproof and waterproof cloth with an internal quilted wool lining and a fitted hood were used, with draw strings to pull tight the waist band, waist and hood. The suit was completely reversible, being finished in white one side and in 'water' or 'splinter' pattern camouflage on the other. The white side was, of course, intended specifically for wear in the snow. On the arms of the white side provision was made (in the form of small buttons) for fastening coloured cloth identity strips which were used to distinguish friend from foe when both sides were wearing white in the snow. Some suits were issued in field grey instead of the camouflage finish.

MISCELLANEOUS CLOTHING

Apart from the various types and orders of dress outlined already, there were other garments of a specialised nature, some of which are

ABOVE: Motor-cyclists wearing the standard rubberised waterproof grey coat issued to motorised troops. This long garment strapped round the lower leg to give optimum weather protection.

BELOW: Mechanics recovering wrecked French tanks in France, 1940. They are wearing standard issue field grey overalls, a one-piece garment of conventional design. Man in background, however, wears the pre-war issue white fatigue suit, a two-piece shapeless coat and trouser combination which the overalls replaced. The overalls had loops for the attachment of the normal uniform shoulder straps though these were not always worn with this garment.

RIGHT: In peacetime training the white fatigue suit was sometimes worn for manoeuvres—or the trousers were often worn in combination with the service tunic as shown here. This assault engineer was pictured so attired during the invasion of France, May 1940. BELOW: White helmet covers worn in Russsia, November 1941. The nearest two men are wearing sheepskin coats, the others greatcoats.

briefly outlined and illustrated here.

Motor Cycle Coat: Issued to men of motor cycle companies and battalions, this was a long, rubberised grey green garment which buttoned close round each leg and had a double-breasted high-cut front. A lighter version also existed for summer wear when the tropical uniform was worn.

Drill Fatigue Dress: A pre-war issue suit was the white denim fatigue dress, worn for drills, exercises and dirty work. It consisted of rather

ABOVE: The heavy sheepskin coat was issued to sentries and front line troops in the early part of the war. These men on the Western Front, early 1940, wear toques, mittens (left) and heavy winter straw lined boots (right) all standard issue. They are wearing the old 1915 pattern steel helmet with prominent lugs originally intended for fitting a sniper's visor. This pattern helmet was deeper than the 1935 pattern.

loose fitting trousers and a loose single-breasted jacket. After 1940 it was rarely issued but the garments continued in use. Sometimes the trousers could be seen worn with the normal field grey tunic in the field while engineer and construction companies might wear all or part of the suit on duties, like bridge construction, road building, or vehicle maintenance. The wartime replacement for the fatigue dress was the field grey overall suit.

Skin Overcoats: For wear in very cold conditions, men on sentry or driver duty and the like could be issued with thick sheep-skin overcoats, worn with the fur inside. There was some pattern variation in the garment and assorted types of skin were used. With the skin

ABOVE: The Army pattern national emblem worn on the right breast of the service tunic and on the cap. It was woven in silver-grey thread on a dark green backing (yellow on brown in tropical version). LEFT: Two toques worn in the most common combination for cold weather protection. Helmet or cap was usually worn over the toques.

overcoat thick leather wool-lined overboots were sometimes worn as well.

Toques, Gloves, Scarf: These winter clothing items were all knitted in heavy gauge field grey colour wool. The toque was a long scarf wrapped round the head to protect the ears and cheeks. One (or more) toques could be used as required.

ARMY RANKS AND INSIGNIA

National Emblems: The national emblem, worn on the right breast of tunics in all orders of dress (but not camouflage clothing) was an eagle badge, the *Hoheitzabzeichen,* which was woven in silver white thread on a very dark bottle green backing. On the tropical dress however, as worn in North Africa the emblem was grey on a light tan cloth backing. For colonels, the emblem was silver and for generals it was gold, again on the tan cloth backing. On forage caps, the Hoheitzabzeichen was worn on the front above a national cockade *(Reichskokarde)* of red/white/black (the national colours). The service cap featured the Hoheitzabzeichen above the Reichskokarde, the latter within a laurel wreath design.

On steel helmets there were two decals, the national emblem (red/white/black shield) on the right side, and an Army emblem (a silver eagle on a black shield) on the left. In 1940 these were discontinued though helmets so marked continued in use for sometime afterwards.

In the last two years of the war, when materials were short, an inferior quality Hoheitzabzeichen came into use, printed or embroidered on a dark grey cloth background which was cut in a simple triangular shape, apex downwards.

Rank Badges: Rank was mainly indicated by devices worn on the shoulder straps, though junior NCOs also wore arm badges. The badges are shown on the accompanying chart. For all enlisted men the shoulder straps and arm badges were faced in a dark bottle green material.

Privates and junior NCOs had plain shoulder straps decorated only with their arm-of-service colour (see below). Unteroffiziers (sergeants), had an open ended braid decoration, while all other NCOs had a braid surround all around the strap. This braid, was 9 mm wide. Until 1939 the shoulder strap also carried a cypher (in varied styles) indicating the regiment or unit, for example 7 for the 7th Regiment. Some regiments also had 'tradition' badges, carried over as a vestige

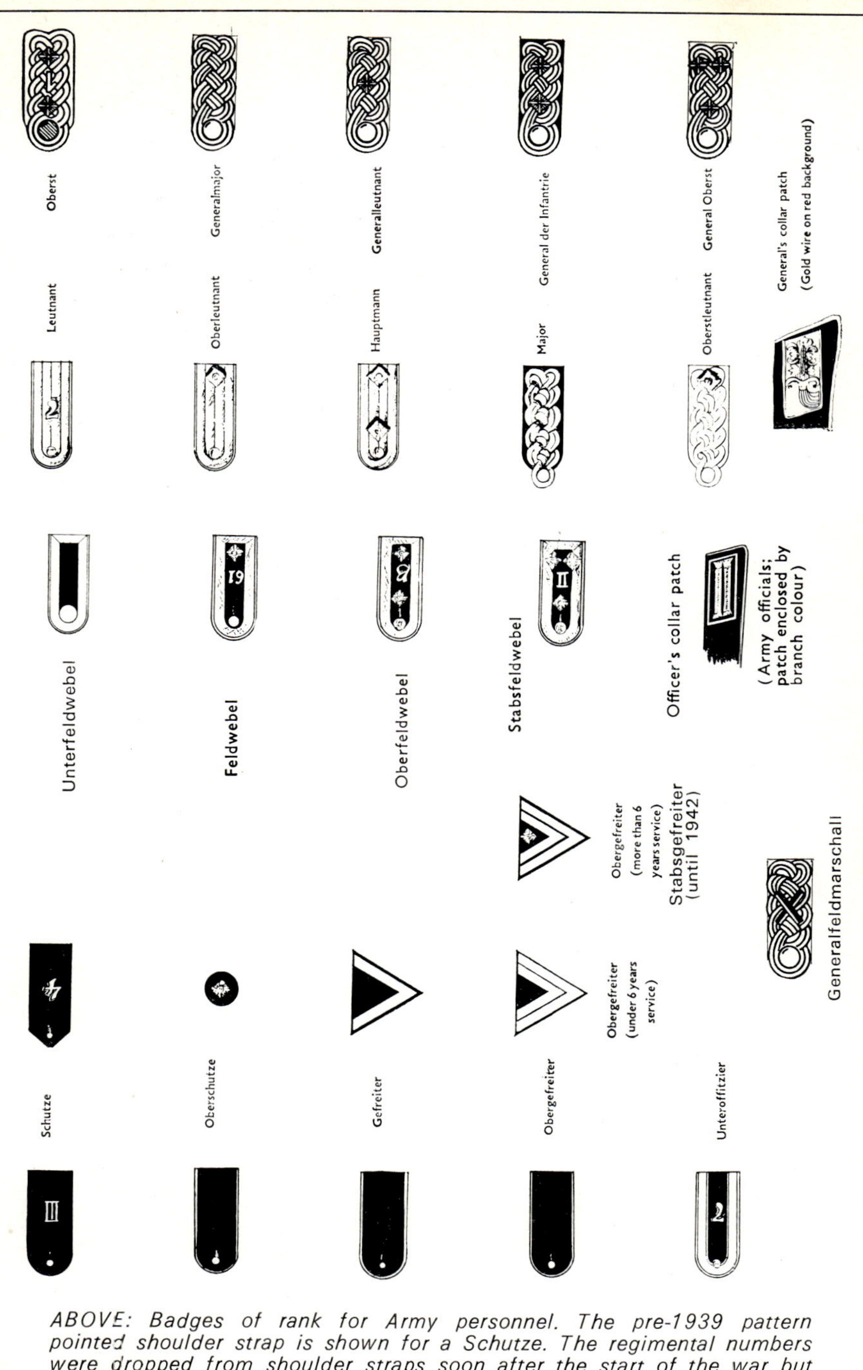

ABOVE: Badges of rank for Army personnel. The pre-1939 pattern pointed shoulder strap is shown for a Schutze. The regimental numbers were dropped from shoulder straps soon after the start of the war but examples are shown. The 'star' for an Oberschutze and chevrons for the Gefreiter and Obergefreiter were worn on the left upper arm.

RIGHT: This Leutnant wears the 1935 pattern helmet with Army eagle decal. The silver lace officer's shoulder straps and collar patches are well shown. Just visible is the white infantry Waffenfarbe round the edges of the shoulder straps (IWM-JMH 141).

of Imperial German Army days (eg 5th Cavalry had a small 'death's head' device having formerly been a 'Death's Head Hussar' regiment). The shoulder strap button also carried a number indicating the company, squadron, or platoon within the unit. On the outbreak of war in 1939, all these identifying devices were dropped for security reasons and plain shoulder straps were ordered. However, some units managed to retain their identity devices for sometime afterwards. The shoulder straps were detachable for cleaning and were not always worn. In the latter part of the war, when economies were enforced, the 1943 pattern tunic was often issued with plain field grey shoulder straps on which the braid and other rank badges were affixed direct. The original shoulder strap design had a blunt pointed end, but in 1938-39 a rounded end was introduced. The older type of shoulder strap was still to be seen however, well into the war.

Officers' shoulder straps were in silver braid being either edged with or backed by (Majors and above) the arm of service colour. Until 1939, unit identity devices were carried, as for the enlisted men.

Arm-of-Service Colcurs: The arm of service (or branch) was indicated by a range of colours known as *Waffenfarben* (short for Waffengatungsfarbe) which means 'arm of service' colour. This had been a traditional means of showing the branch on German uniforms for many years. Enlisted men wore this in the form of piping round their shoulder straps, and on the forage cap in the form of a chevron shaped pattern above the national cockade.

The collar of the Army tunic featured a twin-bar of woven silver grey thread, the whole being incorporated on a backing patch. A central strip in each bar was woven in the German Waffenfarbe colour, this style of lace being known as *Doppelitze.* After 1940 these colour strips were discarded and the bars remained plain silver grey. Officers wore silver braid and many retained the Doppelitze after 1940 on uniforms purchased from military tailors. In the latter part of the war, particularly in conjunction with the 1943 and 1944 pattern tunics, an inferior type of collar patch was issued which consisted of grey woven bars on thin grey cloth backing. The collar of the tunic was faced in dark bottle green cloth and officers wore Waffenfarbe as an edging to the collar. Senior NCOs (unteroffizier, and above) wore 9 mm wide silver grey braid round the edge of collar in service dress. On the 1943 and 1944 pattern tunics, the dark green facing material was often omitted from the collar, and lacing and Waffenfarbe (as appropriate to the rank) were worn directly on the plain field grey collar. A list of the main Waffenfarbe colours is given below.

Arm of Service	**Colour**
Infantry	White
Armoured Troops, Anti-Tank Units, Armoured Reconnaissance Units	Pink
Cavalry	Golden Yellow
Artillery	Bright Red
General Staff Officers	Carmine Red
Signals	Lemon Yellow
Administrative Officials	Dark Green
Engineers	Black
Panzer Grenadiers	Apple Green
Mountain and Jäger Regiments	Light Green
Medical Corps	Cornflower Blue
Mechanised Supply Troops	Light Blue
Recruiting Officers	Orange
Smoke Troops (Rocket Projectors)	Wine Red
Specialist Officers	Grey-Blue
Veterinary Corps	Crimson
Chaplains	Violet
Generals	Bright Red
Military Police	Orange-Red
Armoured Engineers	Black/White

NB: Deviations from regulations included white, pink, or golden yellow for some Panzer-Grenadier units, and pink, golden yellow, or copper brown, for armoured reconnaissance units.

General Officers: Generals wore gilt tunic buttons and gold woven national insignia, as well as the ornate gold lace shoulder straps and collar patches. Trousers featured scarlet stripes up the outer seam, two wide ones flanking piping in the same colour.

Specialist Badges: Special skills or functions for which individual enlisted men or NCOs were qualified were indicated by small badges, mostly worn on the lower part of the right sleeve. In most cases the badges were woven in yellow on a dark green background, but exceptions are noted in the selection of the most common badges given here:

Medical personnel
(Sanitätsunterpersonal)

Fortification maintenance sergeant
(Wallmeister)

Saddler candidate
(Truppensattlermeister-Anwärter)

Paymaster candidate
(Anwärter für die Heeres-Zahlmeisterlaufbahn)

Motor maintenance sergeant (harness sergeant if horse outfit)
(Schirrmeister)

Horseshoeing instructor
(Hufbeschlaglehrmeister)

Horseshoers (personnel)
(Hufbeschlagpersonal)

Radio sergeant
(Funkmeister)

Ordnance sergeant
(Waffenmeister)

Pigeoneer (sergeant)
(Brieftaubenmeister)

Pyrotechnician
(Feuerwerker)

Fortification construction sergeant
(Festungspionier-Feldwebel)

Helmsman (Steuermann). This insignia is worn on the *left upper* sleeve. (Anchor in silver embroidery)

Operator smoke troops (Bedienungspersonal Nebelabteilung). This insignia is worn on the *left lower* arm. Worked in white rayon on dark green background

Communication personnel (other than Signal Corps) (Nachrichtenpersonal). This insignia is worn on the *left upper* sleeve. (Flash in "Waffenfarben")

Army mountain guide (Heeresbergführer). This insignia is worn on the *left breast*

Gunlayer artillery (Richtkanonier). This insignia is worn on *left lower* arm

RIGHT: Feldgendarmes—or military police—carried out traffic control and disciplinary work. They wore normal Army pattern uniform but had the German police escutcheon replacing the normal national insignia on the cap, and on the left sleeve. On duty they wore a distinctive gorget plate carrying the police escutcheon. This plate was luminous to assist night visibility. It could also be worn by any other troops detailed off for regimental police duties.

BELOW: The Feldgendarmerie gorget plate worn by a senior NCO on duty (IWM-MH13104).

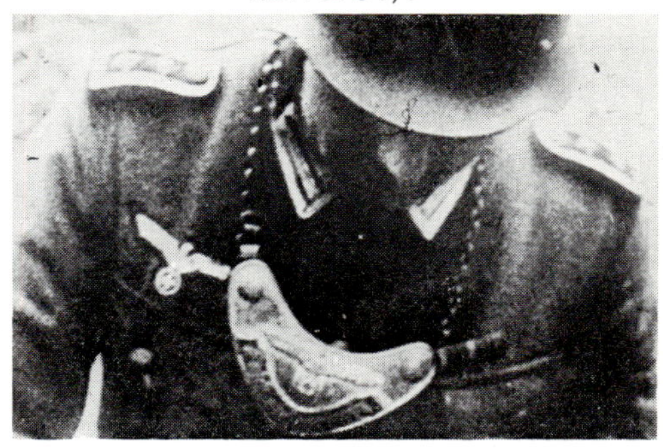

LEFT: Unteroffizier of signal troops in 1940. Yellow Waffenfarbe and silver braid of an Unteroffizier give the illusion of very wide braiding. Note the 1916 pattern helmet. The specialist badge of a pigeon handler can be seen on the lower right sleeve (see opposite).

2: The Armed SS (Waffen - SS)

The 1939 pattern SS-VT field grey uniform is here seen to advantage worn by Sepp Dietrich (centre) who, as an Obergruppenführer, commanded 'Liebstandarte Adolf Hitler' during the invasion of Poland, September 1939. With two staff officers, Dietrich is observing a tank advance. Note the slant side pockets, plain collars, and SS decals on the helmet. The silver lace chevron on the right sleeve indicates SS or NSDAP membership prior to 1933 and is not connected with rank.

LEFT: The SS-VT 1937 pattern field grey service dress, worn by an Unterscharführer. Points to note are the plain collar with black/white twist piping, the black collar patches and shoulder straps, the 'LAH' monogram on the shoulder straps (this was dropped in the first year of the war), the 'Adolf Hitler' cuff title, denoting 'Liebstandarte Adolf Hitler', and the enlisted mens' service cap with death's head device. The slant side pocket is a ready way of identifying the pattern. ABOVE: Men of Standarte No 2 ('Germania' Regiment) in France, May 1940, wearing Army pattern field grey service dress. Note plain collars devoid of the usual collar patches, and national eagle emblem on arm. Unterscharführer on right. Folded smocks carried in belts (IWM-STT1599).

THE Waffen-SS was in effect the 'private army' of the National Socialist Party and it had been built up during the 1930s as an armed élite, initially to guard the Führer and party chiefs. By 1939, still known under its original title as SS-Verfügungstruppen (SS-VT or 'armed reserved troops') the organisation had built up into a sizeable fighting force of 12 regiments. In 1939, they were subsequently organised into divisions on a similar basis to the Army. The Waffen-SS title was adopted during 1940. From 1940 onwards, Waffen-SS

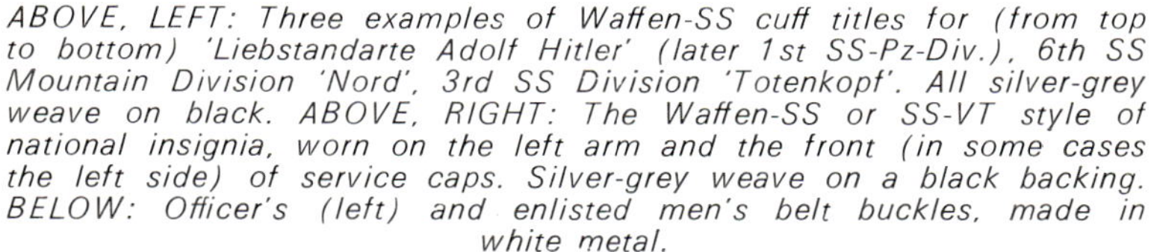

ABOVE, LEFT: Three examples of Waffen-SS cuff titles for (from top to bottom) 'Liebstandarte Adolf Hitler' (later 1st SS-Pz-Div.), 6th SS Mountain Division 'Nord', 3rd SS Division 'Totenkopf'. All silver-grey weave on black. ABOVE, RIGHT: The Waffen-SS or SS-VT style of national insignia, worn on the left arm and the front (in some cases the left side) of service caps. Silver-grey weave on a black backing. BELOW: Officer's (left) and enlisted men's belt buckles, made in white metal.

grew into a huge fighting force. Included on its strength was a Polizeidivision, made up of a police force personnel, organised as a military unit, and numerous divisions of volunteers (Freiwilligen) from the countries which came under German rule from 1940 onwards.

The pre-war SS-VT had a stylish distinctively cut, 'earth grey' service dress—a slightly tawny mid-grey colour—with an open collar tunic which was worn with a brown or grey shirt and a black tie. By 1939 a new field grey 1937 pattern tunic had been issued retaining the style of the earth grey tunic but was slightly simplified. It had a four-button front and a turn-back collar so that it could be worn with the shirt and tie for formal occasions and 'walking out'. A hook or flap fastening on the tunic collar allowed the coat to be buttoned to the neck on active service or in bad weather. This tunic had patch pockets on the breast and slanted slit pockets in the front skirts. The cuffs were plain and the collar had black and white piping and black patches each side. When the SS-VT underwent its major expansion in 1939-40, however, the ordinary Army pattern (ie, 1936 pattern) service dress was adopted for the new units. This dress also replaced the old earth grey service dress and the SS pattern field grey dress in the existing regiments; but in 1940 a few examples of both the old grey service dress and the SS field grey service dress were still to be seen in wear. In general, however, for the duration of the war the Waffen-SS wore the same dress pattern as the Army, with all the varied basic changes described in Part 1.

The major difference was in the provision of badges and insignia which were quite different from the Army system. A big distinction which immediately identified the Waffen-SS was the wearing of the national emblem on the left arm rather than on the right breast as in the Army. The collar, shoulder straps and badge backings, were black rather than dark green. The Waffen-SS also had a system of identifying divisions (and some individual élite units) by cuff titles worn on the left cuff, 15 cm from the bottom edge. The cuff titles were in black with lettering in silver grey weave. One division, 'Totenkopf', had a silver weave death's head device instead of an actual title at one period. The Waffen-SS had its own system of ranks and titles, and its own system of badges which identified ranks by their collar patches as well as the shoulder straps. These are all illustrated in the chart on the next page. The Waffen-SS also had some differences in Waffenfarbe colours, variations being as follows:

Arm of Service	**Colour**
Cavalry and Motorised Reconnaissance Units	Golden Yellow
Tank and Anti-Tank Troops	Rose Pink
Artillery	Bright Red
Infantry	White
General Officers	Light Grey
Concentration Camp Guards	Light Brown
Veterinary Corps	Crimson
Rifle Regiments of SS Police Divisions	Grass Green
Mountain Infantry	Light Green
Administration	Sky Blue
Engineers	Black
Reserve Officers	Dark Green

Other branches had Waffenfarbe colours as for the Army. As the Waffen-SS had its own command and staff structure, and its own commissariat branch, there were several items of combat uniform dress which were peculiar to the Waffen-SS alone and were in no way connected with Army pattern clothing. In some ways, notably in the provision of camouflage clothing, the Waffen-SS were the innovators whose ideas obviously inspired Army thinking.

Headwear: The Waffen-SS wore the same pattern helmet as the Army but had different decal markings. A shield in white with the runic symbol SS was worn on the right while on the left was a red shield with Swastikas in the style of the German national flag. Helmet insignia was dropped around 1941, but continued to be worn for some time. The service cap featured the Waffen-SS death's head badge surmounted by the Waffen-SS national eagle. The pattern of the 1937 service cap differed in small details from the Army equivalent but was generally similar for the respective ranks, and was otherwise styled as described in Part 1.

The national eagle, and the death's head badges were similarly worn on the fronts of the Feldmütze, Gebirgsmütze and Einheitsmütze caps, which were similar to Army pattern. Sometimes the national eagle was worn on the left side of the cap matching the arm position, leaving only the death's head badge at the front. In 1939 a Feldmütze was adopted similar to the Luftwaffe pattern but in field grey material.

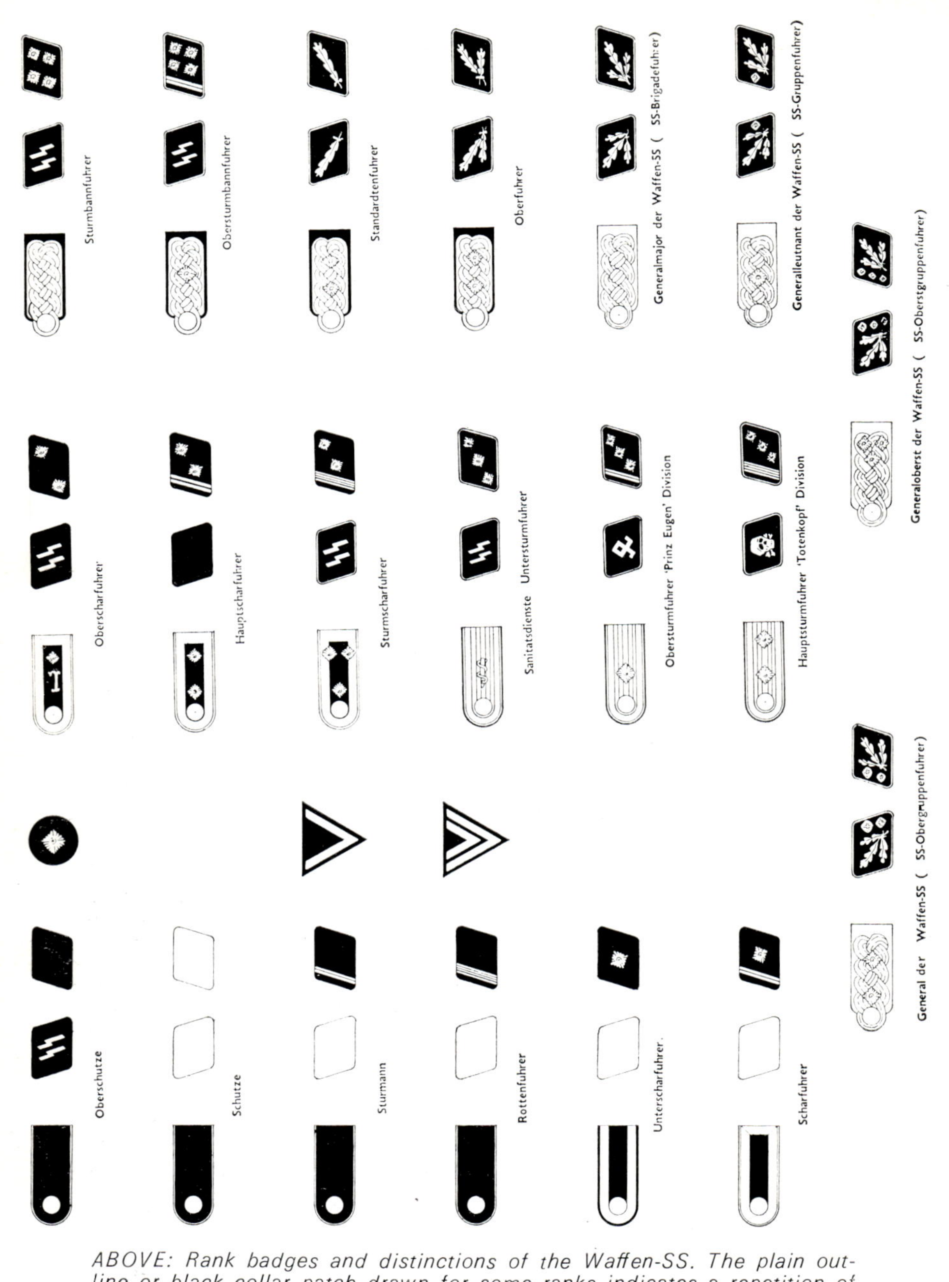

ABOVE: Rank badges and distinctions of the Waffen-SS. The plain outline or black collar patch drawn for some ranks indicates a repetition of the collar patch immediately above. Note that certain divisions wore a distinctive collar patch emblem in place of the runic SS symbol, and two examples are shown. From Standardtenführer upwards, rank badges were worn on both collar patches The 'star' of the Oberschutze and chevrons of the Sturmmann and Rottenführer were worn on the left upper arm.

SS-VT
Signals
Battalion

SS-VT
Assault Engineer
Battalion

SS-VT
Administration
School

SS-VT
Nurnberg Battalion

Early pattern SS-VT collar patches included symbols indicating the unit but these had been dropped by 1940. Some examples are shown here.

On the caps senior officers had silver piping (from Oberführer upwards and junior officers had only white piping officially, but junior officers often wore silver piping too.

Some of the foreign volunteer divisions in the Waffen-SS wore their own style of national head-dress (with Waffen-SS badges) in place of the normal head wear. For example, men of the 13th 'Handschar'

Some volunteer (Freiwilligen) Waffen-SS divisions of foreign nationals wore head dress characteristic of their native lands. These men are of 13th SS-Mountain Division 'Handschar' which was composed of Croatian Moslems. The fez was moss green for enlisted men and deep red for officers. Himmler (left) inspecting these men is in the uniform of a SS general, wearing the leather greatcoat.

The standard SS-VT and Waffen-SS camouflage smock had a characteristic 'mottle' or 'dapple' pattern. Here it is shown worn over a man's equipment. The matching helmet cover is secured to the helmet with metal clips. This light machine gun team in France, May 1940, have an ex-Czech LK gun with which the Germans supplemented their own stocks of weapons.

Division (Croat Moslems) wore a fez.

Camouflage Clothing: Camouflage combat clothing was in use from early 1940—with limited production in 1939. First issue was a camouflage smock and a matching helmet cover with securing metal clips. The smock was reversible, laced at the neck, elasticated at the cuffs and had no collar. These garments came with two styles of 'mottle' (speckled camouflage) quite distinct from the Army 'water' and 'splinter' patterns. One side was in predominately greens for spring and summer wear, while the other was in browns for fall and winter wear. There were at least eight, probably more, patterns of 'mottle' type Waffen-SS camouflage. Later smocks had loops added for the fixing of local foliage if necessary, and some had external pockets in addition to the side slits which gave the wearer access to inner pockets.

In mid 1943 a complete camouflage suit was issued. Made of cheap drill material it was closely patterned on the cut of the normal service dress. Several different 'mottle' pattern camouflages were used. Badges were not officially permitted on this suit, but in practice they were generally worn. A further camouflage suit was a version of the special double-breasted tank suit in 'mottle' pattern drill. Also issued to AFV crews was a 'mottle' pattern one-piece overall suit. This buttoned down the front and was worn with a waist belt. Some artillery men were also issued with these camouflaged overalls. A fully camouflaged forage cap (based in style on the einheitsmütze) was issued from 1942 and became common wear for

ABOVE: The feldmütze of the Waffen-SS on common issue was similar in style to the Luftwaffe version. The national insignia was usually, (but not always) worn on the side as shown here. These men are engineers on bridge building work and are wearing the standard smock.

LEFT: Local foliage was attached to the helmet cover for added concealment. With smock and mottle-painted rocket launcher (RP43), this infantryman merges well with the undergrowth as he waits for approaching enemy tanks, Normandy, June 1944.

ABOVE: Under active service conditions there was great variety in the way of wearing personal equipment. When the smock was worn the braces were often discarded and most items were suspended from the belt, except for the anti-gas respirator case which had its own sling. Note man on right with trousers outside his jackboots (IWM-MH 12867). LEFT: The assault engineer at Normandy in June 1944 demonstrates how well his 'mottled' helmet cover and smock matches the adjacent foliage. Seated at left with a Panzerfaust is a paratrooper.

LEFT: Close view of the Waffen-SS smock showing its elasticated cuffs. It lacked a collar and the tunic collar showed outside it. The Waffen-SS also had a camouflaged version of the Einheitsmütze. A later version had side turn up like the field grey cap. Collar patch indicates rank of Sturmann (IWM-STT5714). RIGHT: A face mask in field grey was unique to the Waffen-SS. It secured round the crown of the helmet with a strap. The ends of the sleeves of the smock either hung loose or, as in these pictures, were tucked up inside the elasticated wrists.

combat units. Yet another camouflage item peculiar to the Waffen-SS was a loose hanging face mask designed to be attached to the helmet.

Special low visibility cloth rank badges were introduced for wear with camouflaged clothing as shown in the illustrations on the next page. Subsequently these were also adopted for equivalent ranks in the Army when the latter introduced camouflage clothing in the 1942-43 period.

For winter wear the Waffen-SS used the standard issue items, but one distinct Waffen-SS garment was a lined anorak, neutral grey in colour and with matching trousers. This was semi-fly fronted with full skirt, had patch breast pockets and an attached hood. The Waffen-SS also issued quilted parkas of various styles. In the later war period there were instances of Waffen-SS men wearing Army 'splinter' pattern camouflage garments (and vice versa) but this was not a common occurrence.

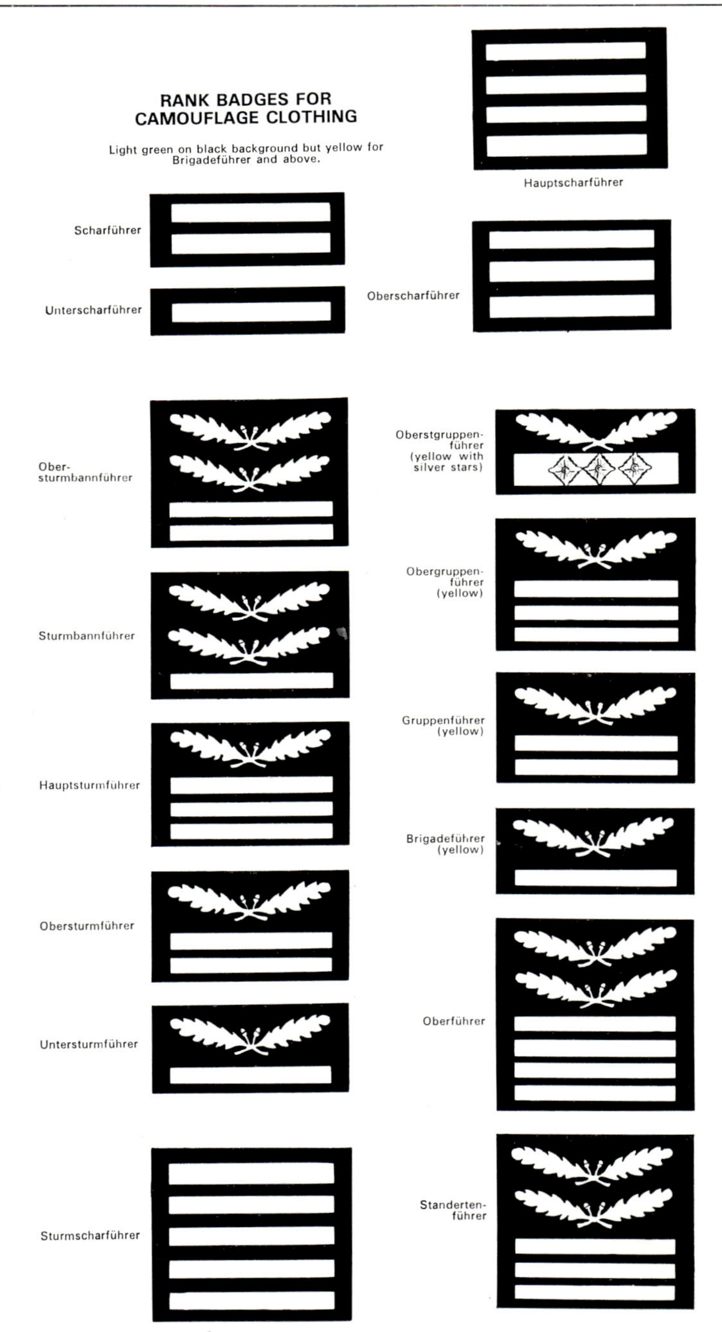

N.B. Same badges for equivalent ranks were worn by Army personnel with camouflage clothing.

ABOVE, LEFT: Here is the face mask shown on page 61 thrown back over the helmet when not needed. This is the crew of a 8·1 cm mortar. Note that they lack helmet covers. RIGHT: In mid 1943 a complete camouflage suit was issued, made in cheap drill material and in a style similar to the normal service dress. Officially no badges were to be worn with this suit but the national insignia was, nonetheless, frequently worn on the left arm. Gaiters and ankle boots were commonly worn in the latter part of the war.

SS Mountain Troops: SS Mountain Troops wore the standard type of clothing issued to Army mountain troops except that the badges and insignia conformed to SS practice for style and position. Climbing boots and short cloth puttees were worn instead of jackboots or ankle boots. The Gebirgsmütze cap was normal wear. The Edelweiss flower badge was worn in the normal positions for this distinctive insignia. In addition to the special clothing of all types (as described in Part 1), Waffen-SS mountain troops could also be seen wearing the SS pattern reversible camouflage smock, the camouflage helmet cover, and the camouflage field cap.

Specialist Badges: Officers and NCOs with special skills wore an extra badge on the left cuff denoting their qualifications. This was a practice copied, in 1942, from the Army (see page 49). The regulation Waffen-SS specialist badge was a small black cloth diamond with the symbol woven in grey or silver-grey thread. Some of the more common specialist badges are shown below, but there were many more. Due to shortages in the last couple of years of the war, however, the equivalent Army specialist badges were sometimes worn by the SS personnel.

General Officers: Extra distinctions for the service dress of officers of general's rank were pale grey facings to the revers of the greatcoat, shown by leaving the top buttons undone, and a 'triple' stripe—two wide, one narrow—down the outside seam of the trousers or breeches. These stripes were in white and were a late introduction fashioned after the style of red stripes worn by Army generals. The SS originally wore an earth grey greatcoat with collar patches but from 1940 this was replaced by the Army pattern field grey garment.

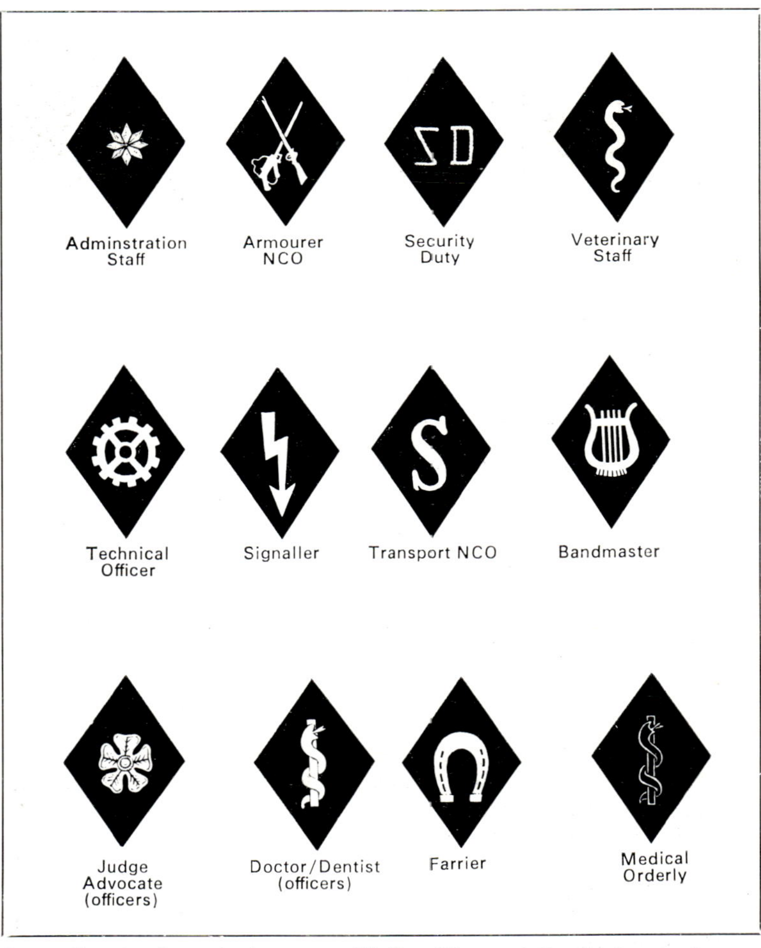

A small selection of the many Waffen-SS specialist badges, all worn above the left cuff.

ABOVE: A variety of different styles of combat clothing is being worn by the crew of this Waffen-SS Sd Kfz 10/5 flak vehicle in 1944. Man on left wears the Einheitsmütze cap. Man second left wears the reed green tropical trousers, and all wear a mixture of jackboots and ankle boots. BELOW: The field grey wool scarf is worn by this NCO in the Ardennes, 1944. He carries a captured American M1 carbine , and has the camouflage smock and helmet cover (IWM-EA48012).

ABOVE: The rubberised waterproof coat for motorised troops is shown left. Note how it secures at the bottom with straps round the legs. Gauntlets were standard issue for motorised troops also seated man wears the Waffen-SS feldmütze and a variation on the sheepskin winter coat with black instead of white fur. LEFT: Quilted parka in field grey was a Waffen-SS item issued to key men on the Russian front like this artillery observation officer.

3 : The Air Force (Luftwaffe) Ground Combat Troops

The Luftwaffe Flakartillerie detachment of a Flakvierling Quad 20 mm AA gun are all wearing the Fliegerbluse except for the commander (with binoculars) who wears the service tunic. Fliegerbluse was shorter than the tunic, lacked patch pockets, and had concealed buttons.

These Luftwaffe Flakartillerie men are guarding a seaplane base in Norway, May 1940. They wear the standard greatcoat, service dress, and Fliegermütze forage cap. Rank patches of an Unteroffizier may be seen on the nearest man.

LUFTWAFFE uniforms in general are beyond the scope of this book, which is devoted solely to those in the ground-fighting and paratroop roles. Luftwaffe service dress was blue-grey in colour, similar in cut to Army dress, though the tunic had a turn back collar. For walking out and for officers this could be worn with a grey shirt and black tie. The collar would also button up to the neck for parade and combat use. The forage cap was of a 'fore and aft' garrison type with shallow turn-ups at the side. The national eagle emblem, worn on the

Mützen-Hoheitsabzeichen Luftwaffe (cap national insignia of air force)

Hoheitsabzeichen für Rock u. Feldbluse (national insignia for coat and field blouse of the air force)

ABOVE, LEFT: National insignia as worn on Luftwaffe service cap. RIGHT: National insignia worn on tunic (US Official).

cap and right breast, was in 'flying' pose and was carried in decal form on the helmet side. The leather belt and equipment was brown before the war, but black equipment replaced it in the early war years. The Luftwaffe Flak units wore the standard Luftwaffe service dress and equipment, as did Luftwaffe units serving as infantry. The alternative garment to the service dress tunic, and very commonly worn, was the Fliegerbluse, a short fly-front jacket originally introduced for air crew. The Fliegerbluse was standard wear (beneath the smock) for paratroops, and was frequent wear for flak troops. It was blue-grey in colour, and rank badge collar patches, plus the Luftwaffe breast eagle were worn

Crew of a 3·7 cm AA gun in Greece display features of the Fliegerbluse. Man in centre wears national insignia, on breast, often omitted from the Fliegerbluse. In this hot climate no undershirt is being worn.

These two views show the service cap and Fliegerbluse as worn by a Paratroop Oberfeldwebel. He wears the paratroop badge on his left breast and a shirt and tie. The junior ranks are wearing brown overalls and the Fliegermütze cap.

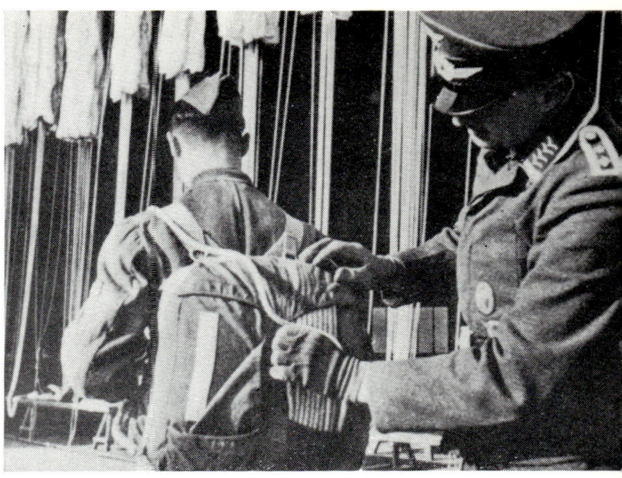

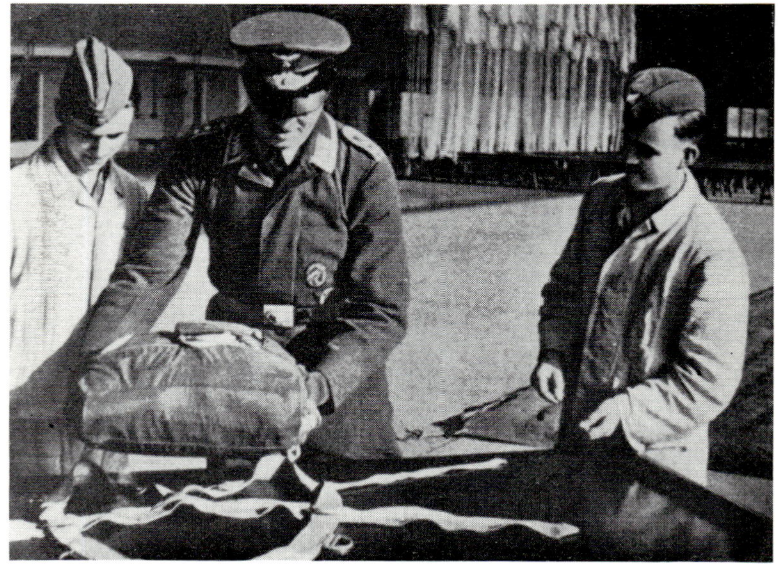

on this garment in the 'standard' positions, though the eagle was not always worn on this jacket.

Ranks were indicated on shoulder straps and collar patches, and piping (and the patches themselves) were coloured to indicate the branch. Small 'wings' were used as rank indicators on the coloured collar patches. For the units with a ground fighting rôle the applicable colours were as follows:

Branch	**Colour**
Anti-aircraft (Flak)	Bright Red
Signals	Golden Brown
General Officers	White
Hermann Goering Panzer Division	White with red edging to patch

RIGHT: Luftwaffe personnel in mountain divisions, like these signallers, wore mountain boots, cloth puttees, and a Luftwaffe blue version of the Gebirgsmütze cap. Later a Luftwaffe version of the Einheitsmütze was introduced. These NCOs are wearing the Fliegerbluse. BELOW: In parade order, paratroops wore their smock and parachute harness over full service dress. These men, at Hitler's 1939 birthday parade wear jackboots and collars and tie. Note the rank badges on the smocks (IWM-MH13114).

Enlisted men had plain collars but senior NCOs had silver braid collar edging and officers had silver braid in addition round their collar patches. Luftwaffe greatcoats were similar in style to the Army, but had plain collars with rank patches on the points. There was also a reed green denim tropical uniform (which washed out to a neutral fabric shade) virtually identical to the Army pattern, but for the badges and badge positions. Ankle boots were worn with this dress and in the latter part of the war it became quite common summer wear in Europe in place of the blue-grey service dress.

Luftwaffe personnel (such as flak and signal units) serving with mountain divisions wore their uniform in mountain troops' style—a gebirgsmütze forage cap, ankle or climbing boots, and canvas puttees. The service tunic or Fliegerbluse was worn as appropriate.

Paratroops: Paratroops were a Luftwaffe committment, the Army paratroops having been transferred to Luftwaffe control in 1939. Originally, the paratroops wore a blue-grey Fliegerbluse over which was worn a rush green (grey-green) smock. This was used in the

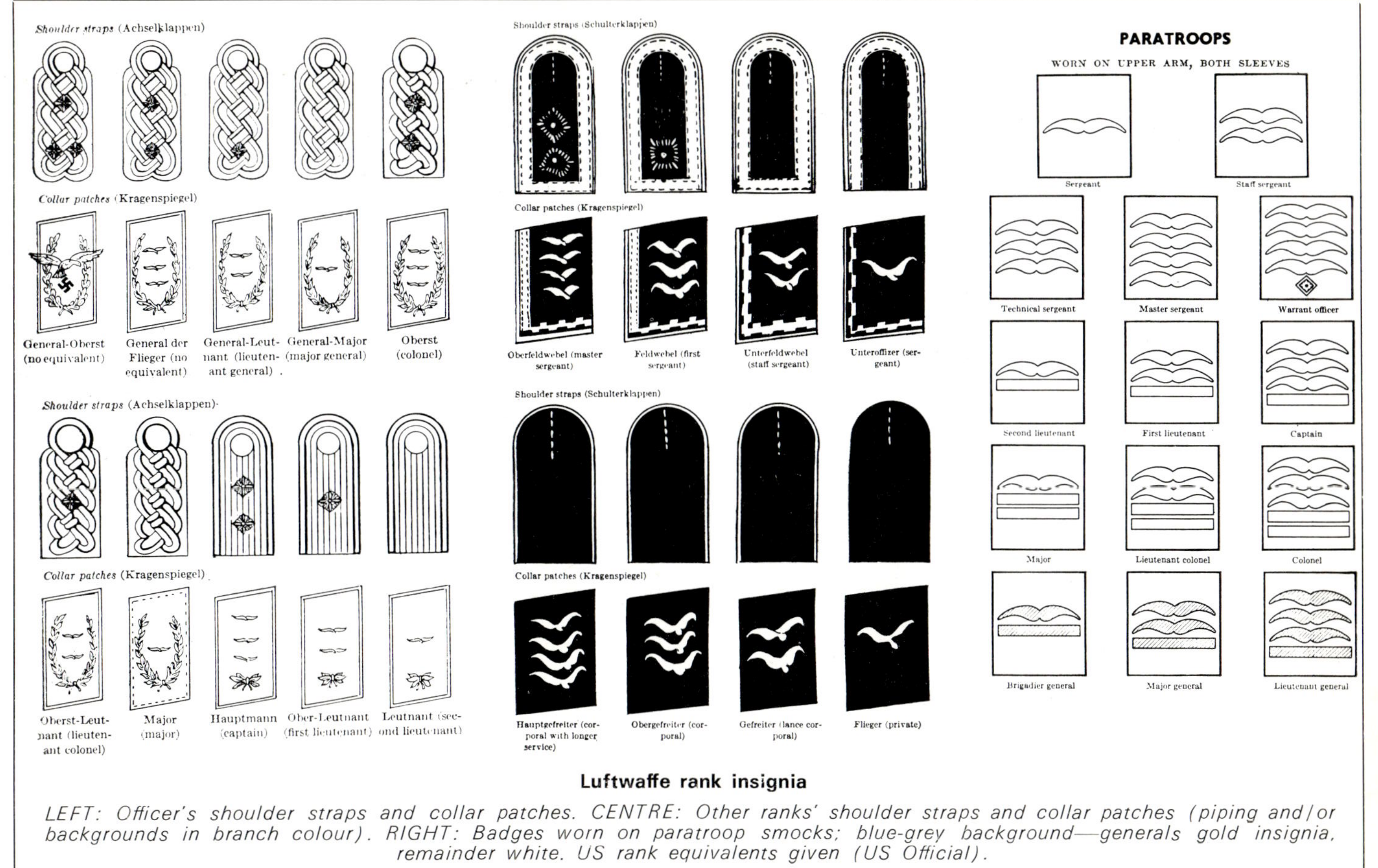

Luftwaffe rank insignia

LEFT: Officer's shoulder straps and collar patches. CENTRE: Other ranks' shoulder straps and collar patches (piping and/or backgrounds in branch colour). RIGHT: Badges worn on paratroop smocks; blue-grey background—generals gold insignia, remainder white. US rank equivalents given (US Official).

ABOVE: Luftwaffe Flakartillerie Gefrieter in greatcoat, service issue gloves, and Fliergermütze cap. Rank patch appeared on collar points, in this case red with silver 'wings'.

1939-41 period. The smock was just over knee length but could be fastened up around the top of the wearer's legs so that the parachute harness would not be fouled when jumping. It had zip breast pockets. Later, a camouflaged smock of similar pattern (but lacking the zip pockets) were issued with a green/brown 'splinter' type pattern. By 1943 most Luftwaffe parachute units were deployed in the ground fighting role (the opportunities for airborne operations having diminished)

BELOW: Paratroops in 1939 on their way to make a demonstration jump for Hitler. They wear full service dress complete with collar and tie. Note the lightweight paratroop helmet which was painted Luftwaffe blue and carried national insignia decals as shown (the shield was red/white/black).

ABOVE: Parachute troops in Holland, May 1940, wearing the service tunic or Fliegerbluse beneath their rush green smock. Most wear shirts open at the neck as well. The helmets are daubed with clay. Man on left wears the Army national insignia, indicating that he is a former Army parachutist. Army parachute units were transferred to Luftwaffe in 1939.

LEFT: Paratroops leaving Ju 52 aircraft at the time of the Crete landings in 1941. Note that the smock is now camouflaged and the helmet of the nearest man is painted to match.

Paratroops in action during the invasion of Crete. Furthest man has a camouflaged smock, and nearest has the rush green type. Note the short jump boots gathering in the trousers at the ankle. BELOW: Paratroops running for cover immediately on landing during the invasion of Holland, May 1940. They have just recovered their weapons from a supply container behind the man on the right.

and a combat dress more suitable for the new role was adopted. This featured a shortened smock in camouflage pattern with the blue-grey Fliegerbluse and either blue-grey service trousers or light-weight summer drill trousers. A camouflage helmet cover was also issued, but the paratroop light-weight helmet was retained by most units. Others had the standard steel helmet, particularly towards the end of the war.

High ankle boots were worn by paratroops but in the later part of the war the ubiquitous ankle boots and canvas anklets became more common.

ABOVE: Paratroops in France in 1944 showing the later type of smock in wear. Well shown here are the knee pads, to protect the knees on landing, usually worn under the trousers but here worn outside them. ABOVE, RIGHT: Drawings show the difference between camouflage smock of 1941-43 period (left) and the shortened type (right) worn by some paratroops in 1944-45. RIGHT: An Unteroffizier in France, 1944 in the earlier type of camouflaged smock. Note rank badge on each arm and net on helmet for affixing local foliage.

LEFT: Paratroops in Crete patrol Suda Bay in a captured British LCA. They wear the normal belt and braces over their jump smocks, and a Fliegermütze cap in place of the helmet. BELOW: Paratroops jumped without their guns at the beginning of the war. These were dropped with them in a container. First task on the ground was to recover their side-arms from the container. These men are in Holland, May 1940. They wear the then current rush green smock.

Like the Waffen-SS, the paratroops had special sleeve badges for wear on combat clothing and these are shown in the accompanying chart, reproduced on page 72.

Special Clothing: For fatigues and dirty work, Luftwaffe personnel were issued with an overall suit. This was a one-piece dark blue garment secured with the waist belt and with rank patches on the turn-down

ABOVE: Overalls were worn for fatigues and as an alternative to the Fliegerbluse by gun crews and Luftwaffe tank crews. This Unteroffizier is from a Luftwaffe tank company on airfield defence work in France. Vehicle is a captured French R 35. RIGHT: Long camouflage coverall worn by an Unteroffitzier of a Luftwaffe infantry unit. He wears service dress with gaiters and ankle boots. The weapon is a captured American M1 carbine.

collar. These overalls were frequently worn in lieu of service dress by tank crews and flakartillerie personnel. Some coveralls were issued in brown rather than blue, and the twill material used to wash out to a much lighter shade over a period of time. Units serving in a ground fighting rôle (ie, as infantry) were issued with several Army items such as camouflage helmet covers and ponchos.

General Officers: Luftwaffe generals wore white 'triple' stripes—two wide, one narrow—on the outside seams of their breeches or trousers. The revers of their greatcoats were also faced in white and were displayed by leaving the top buttons undone.

4: Accoutrements

PERSONAL equipment was virtually the same for all services described in this book. The waistbelt alone could be worn in light order, but braces were usual in fighting order. For marching order a large pack could be carried on the braces suspended from additional straps, this was more usually carried in unit transport, however.

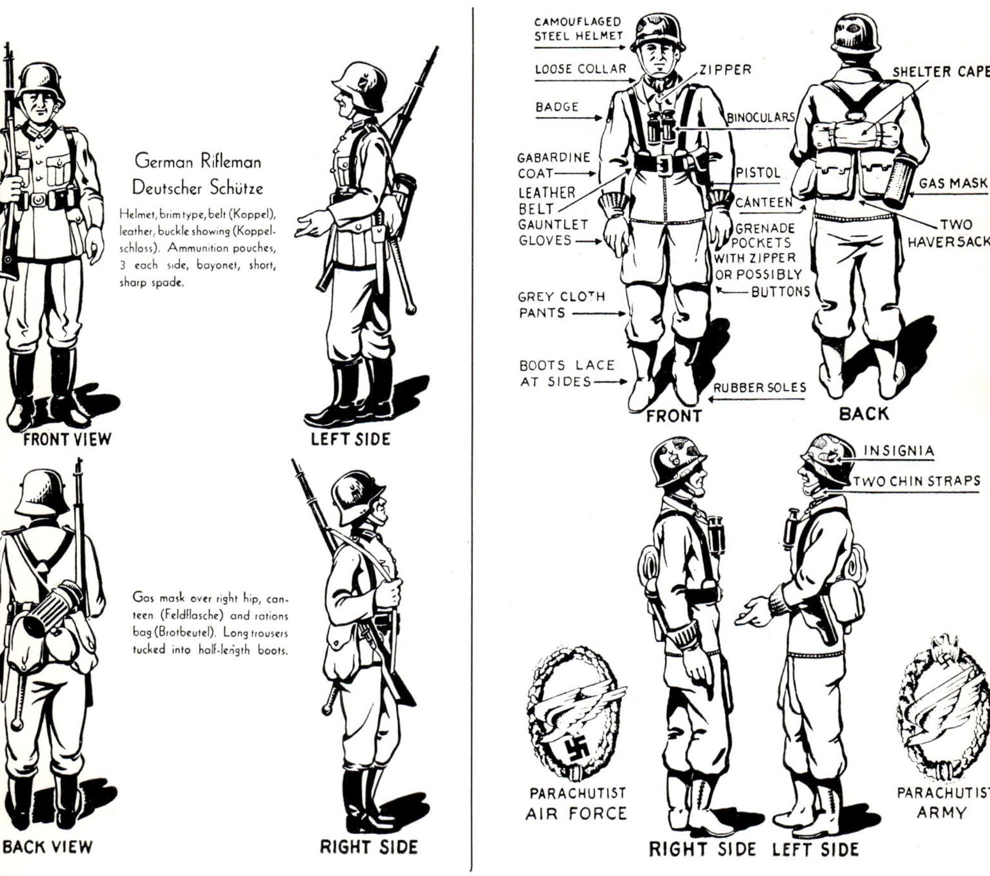

LEFT: Basic personal equipment worn in fighting order by German infantryman. An additional large hide pack (tornister) was worn on the centre of the back, together with rolled greatcoat and poncho when in marching order. RIGHT: Luftwaffe parachute officer or senior NCO in fighting order, 1940 period. Parachutist bardge was worn on left breast of fliegerbluse or service tunic; Army version was obsolete by 1940 (US Official).

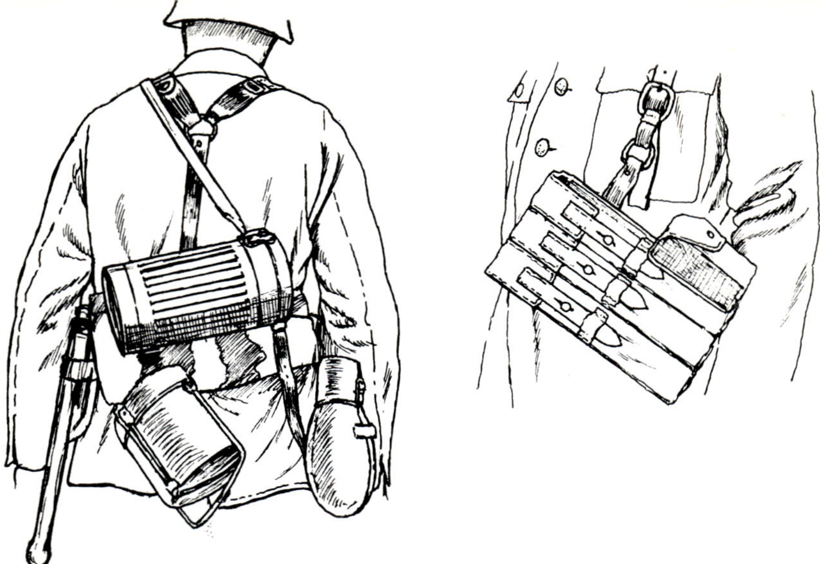

ABOVE, LEFT: The normal method of wearing the belt, braces, and equipment in fighting order. The entrenching tool, canteen, bread bag, water bottle, and folded Zeltbahn were all attached to the belt. ABOVE, RIGHT: The Schmeisser machine pistols, MP 38 and MP 40, required long magazines, and special pouches were supplied for these. They were worn in place of the rifle magazine pouches by men carying these weapons.

A light metal yoke and an assault pack could be attached to the 'D' rings on the braces for carrying extra equipment. This 5 cm mortar crew carry their baseplate and barrel on the metal yoke when on the march. Note Zeltbahn and canteen slung high on braces to allow clearance. MG 34 team carried their folded tripod, etc, in same way.

5 : Decorations

DECORATIONS and awards is a subject in its own right and only brief coverage can be given here. In the Army and Waffen-SS special badges were awarded for skills at arms in the field. The most important are shown and described here. There were other decorations such as the cuff title 'AFRIKA' for Afrika Korps veterans and an armshield to indicate service in the Crimea—plus, of course the more conventional campaign medals for which ribbons were awarded.

RIGHT: A much decorated Unteroffizier wearing a Close Combat Clasp in silver on his left breast above the pocket and two Tank Destruction badges on his right sleeve. This special decoration was awarded for the single-handed destruction of a tank by use of normal infantry weapons only; the badge was an aluminium-coloured ribbon with black edging and a bronze coloured miniature tank emblem. On his breast, partly obscured, this soldier is also wearing either the Infantry Assault badge or the similar Tank Assault badge which are both shown on the next page. BELOW: The 'Afrika Korps' cuff title and the 'Afrika' title awarded later to DAK veterans—they were not actually worn simultaneously. (Photo-War).

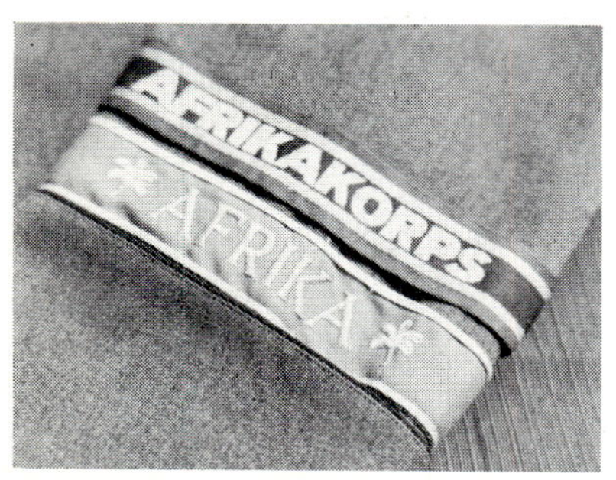

BELOW, LEFT: Detail of Tank Destruction badge. BELOW: Detail of Close Combat Clasp.

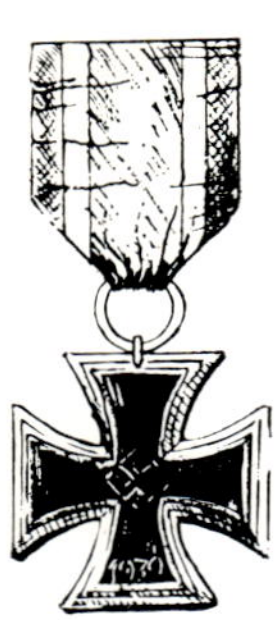

ABOVE LEFT: The Iron Cross 2nd Class was the most widely awarded of the four classes of Iron Cross. The swasktika and date 1939 distinguished it from the World War 1 Iron Cross. The ribbon of dark red flanked with white and black bars was normally worn in the second button hole of the tunic in service dress, the cross itself not being worn. ABOVE CENTRE: Panzer unit marksmanship shield (awarded to AFV gunners). ABOVE RIGHT: Infantry Assault Badge worn on left breast; awarded for three successful attacks on different days. LEFT: Tank Assault Badge. Awarded initially for 3 successful actions but from July 1943 extra grades were issued for 25, 50, 75, and 100 actions. The first grade (25) carried this figure in the knot at the bottom of the wreath.

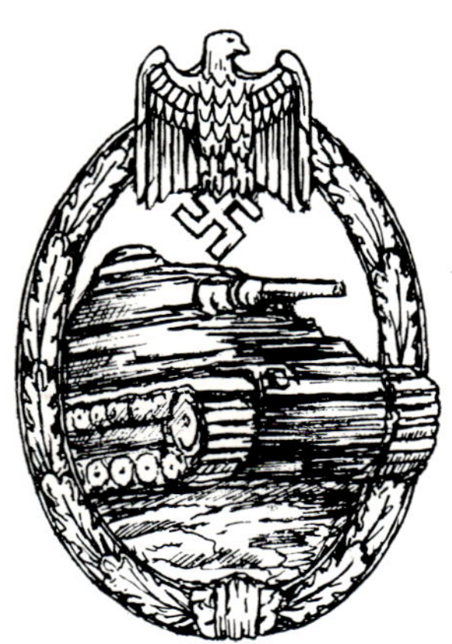

Glossary of Uniform Terms

English	German	Remarks
Pack	Tornister	Canvas with leather binding
Tunic/blouse	Feldbluse	Service tunic
Trousers	Hosen	Service trousers
Greatcoat	Mantel	
Steel helmet	Stahlhelm	1943, 1935 or 1916 pattern
Field cap	Feldmütze	Fore-and-aft type cap
Mountain cap	Bergemütze	Peaked
Field cap (peaked)	Einheitsmütze	Derived from mountain cap, adopted 1943
Field cap (Luftwaffe)	Fleigermütze	Differed from Army pattern
Tank helmet	Schutzmütze	Army until 1940
National insignia	Hoheitzabzeichen (Army/Waffen-SS)	Eagle emblem
	Hoheitszeichen (Luftwaffe)	'Flying' eagle
Rosette (caps)	Reichskokarde	Not in Waffen-SS
Arm of service colour	Waffenfarbe	Piping or lace
Flight coat	Fliegerbluse	Luftwaffe only
Shoulder straps	Schulterklappen	
Service cap	Dienstmütze	

6: Infantry Weapons

DETAILS of German infantry weapons are given in more specialised books, but basic coverage of the most commonly used items is included here to facilitate recognition of the more important pieces. The drawings are *not* to a common scale.

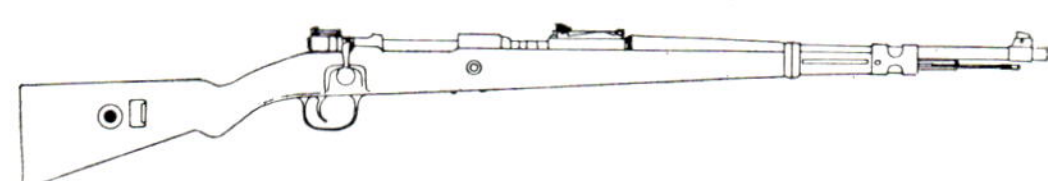

Karbine 98 Kurz (Kar 98K) Mauser

Calibre: *7·92mm (·312 inches).*
Magazine capacity: *5 rounds, internal box magazine.*
Weight: *8 pounds 8 ounces.*
Range: *3,000 yards maximum,*
800 yards effective.
Muzzle velocity: *2,800 fps.*
Sights: *Rear: open, vee-notch tangent graduated from 100 to 2,000 metres.*
Fore: inverted vee-blade which was fixed and could be fitted with a cowl (NB. No facilities for windage adjustments on sights).

This was the standard rifle and is shown in use in many pictures in this book.

Small arms drawings by Kenneth M. Jones

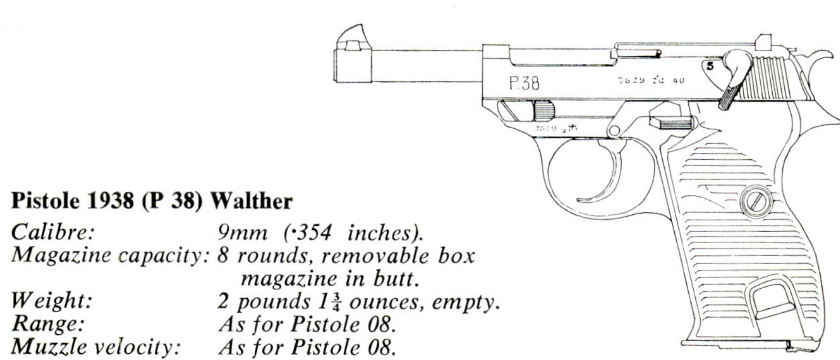

Pistole 1938 (P 38) Walther

Calibre: *9mm (·354 inches).*
Magazine capacity: *8 rounds, removable box magazine in butt.*
Weight: *2 pounds $1\frac{3}{4}$ ounces, empty.*
Range: *As for Pistole 08.*
Muzzle velocity: *As for Pistole 08.*

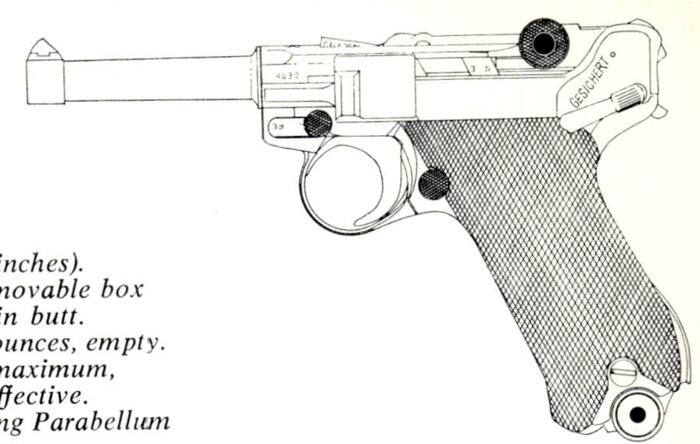

Pistole 1908 (P 08) Luger

Calibre: *9mm (·354 inches).*
Magazine capacity: *8 rounds, removable box magazine in butt.*
Weight: *1 pound 14 ounces, empty.*
Range: *1,150 yards maximum, 25 yards effective.*
Muzzle velocity: *1,040 fps using Parabellum ammunition.*

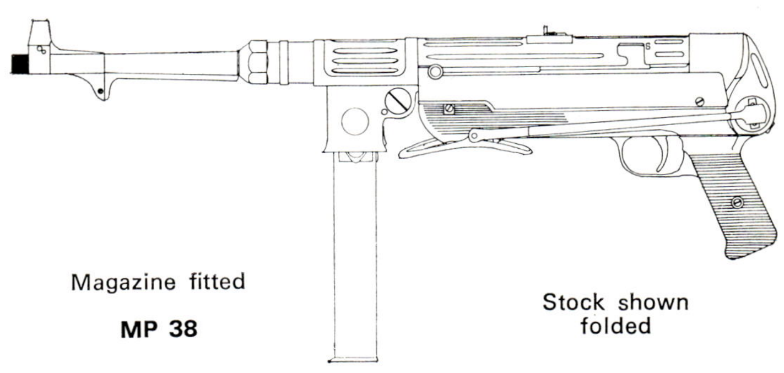

Magazine fitted

MP 38

Stock shown folded

Maschinenpistole 38 & 40 (MP 38 & MP 40)

Calibre: *9mm (·354 inches).*
Magazine capacity: *32 rounds, in removable box magazine.*
Weight: *10 pounds 7 ounces, loaded.*
Range: *1,850 yards maximum, 200 yards effective.*
Rate of fire: *Practical, up to 100 rpm burst fire.*
Sights: *Rear: fixed and folding leaf open notch. fixed, 100 metres, folding, 200 metres.*
Fore: fixed inverted vee-blade with ring cowl cover.

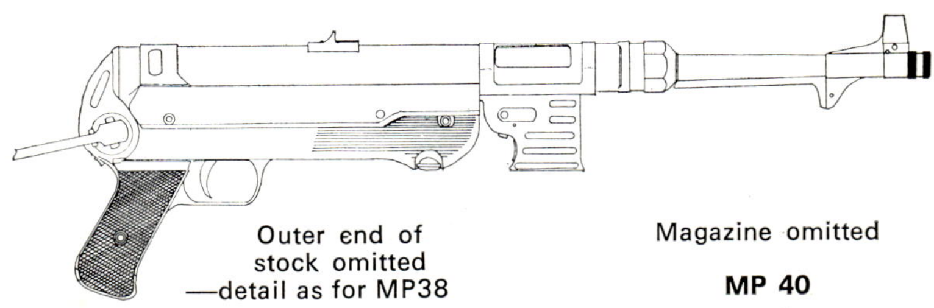

Outer end of stock omitted —detail as for MP38

Magazine omitted

MP 40

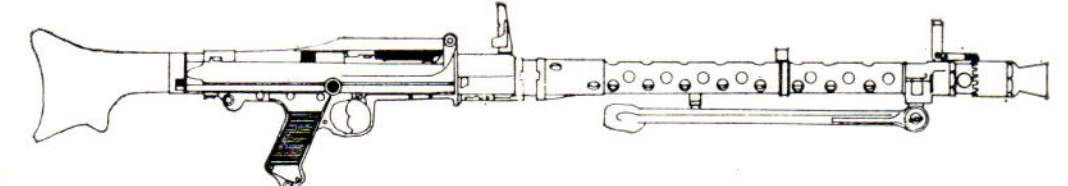

Maschinengewehr 34 (MG 34)

Calibre:	*7·92mm (·312 inches).*
Feed:	*Left side; (1) 50 round interconnecting non-disintergating metallic-link belt. (2) 75 round saddle drum feed. (3) 50 round belts in drums. (4) 100 round canvas containers for tank use.*
Action:	*Semi- and fully-automatic, short recoil action. Air cooled, with barrel changing facility. There is a recoil booster fitted to the end of the barrel which aids barrel recoil by gas pressure force upon the barrel face.*
Weight:	*26 pounds 8 ounces.*
Range:	*5,000 yards maximum, 3,825 yards tripod mounted, 2,000 yards tripod mounted (effective ranges).*
Sights:	*Vertical rear leaf, graduated 200 to 2,000 metres, foresight fixed, inverted vee blade. Telescopic sights for use in the heavy role (when mounted on a tripod) sighted up to 3,500 metres. AA ring sight fitting.*
Muzzle velocity:	*Dependent on ammunition used: up to 3,000 fps. Ammunition used: Ball, AP and AP tracer.*
Rate of fire:	*Approximately 900 rpm cyclic.*

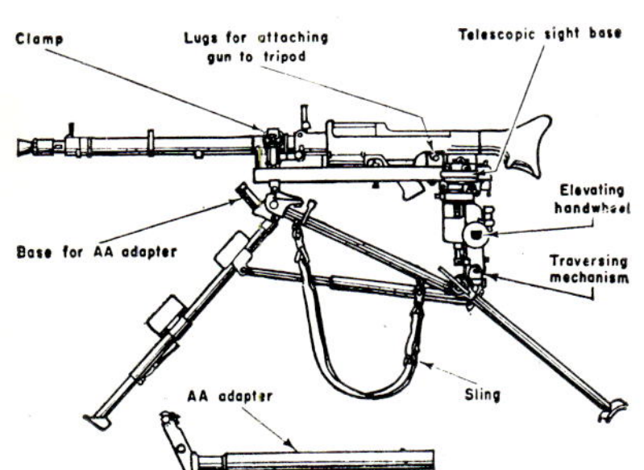

LEFT: A diagram of the MG 34 on the tripod mount. Note carrying sling for folded mount. The same tripod with legs extended and the AA adaptor fitted converted the gun for the anti-aircraft role (US Official).

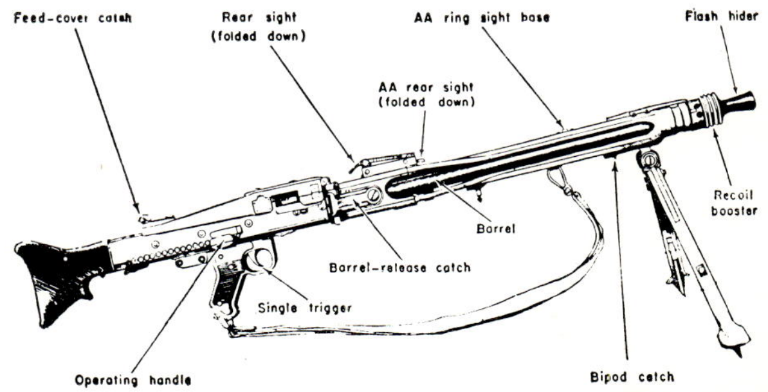

RIGHT: The MG 42 appeared later in the war as a partial replacement for the MG 34. It was similar to the latter but simplified and refined in design. It had a squarer section barrel jacket compared to the MG 34.

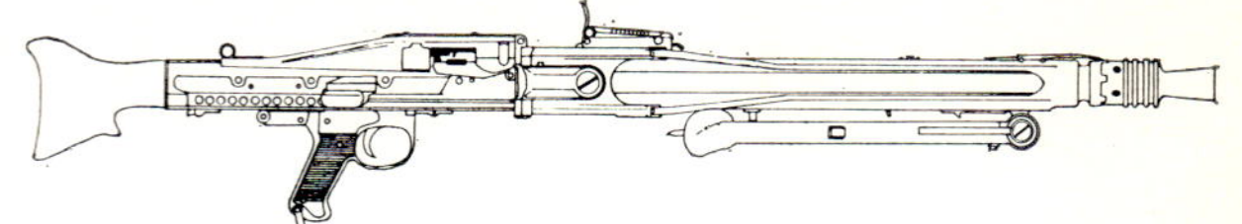

Maschinengewehr 42 (MG 42)

Calibre:	*7·92mm (·312 inches).*
Feed:	*Left side; (1) 50 round interconnecting non-disintergrating metallic-link belts. (2) 50 round belts in drums. (3) 100 round canvas containers for tank use.*
Action:	*Fully automatic only. Combination short recoil blowback action. Air cooled, with barrel changing facility. Fitted with a recoil booster as in the MG 34.*
Weight:	*25 pounds 8 ounces.*
Range:	*Approximately as for MG 34.*
Sights:	*Rear tangent graduated from 200 to 2,000 metres. Anti-aircraft peep sight fitted to rear sight, which was used in conjunction with the standard AA ring sight as used on the MG 34.*
Muzzle velocity:	*Dependent on ammunition used . . . as for MG 34.*
Rate of fire:	*1,300 rpm cyclic (decrease in accuracy compared with the MG 34).*

This gun was intended as a replacement for the MG 34.

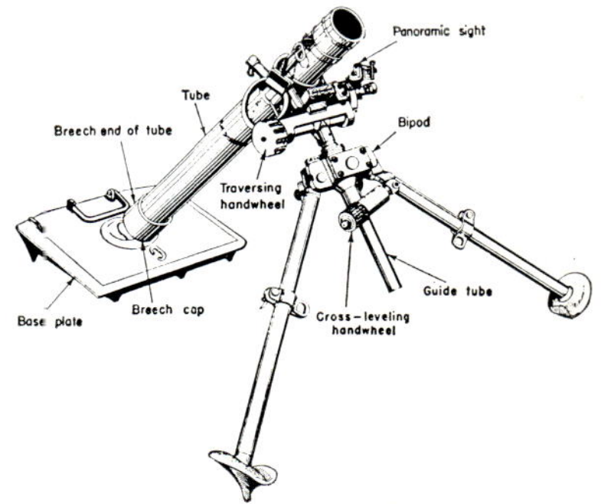

RIGHT: Standard heavy infantry mortar was the 8 cm (81 mm) Gr.W. 34 which had a maximum range of 2,078 yards weighed 125 pounds, and broke into three parts for transportation (US Official).

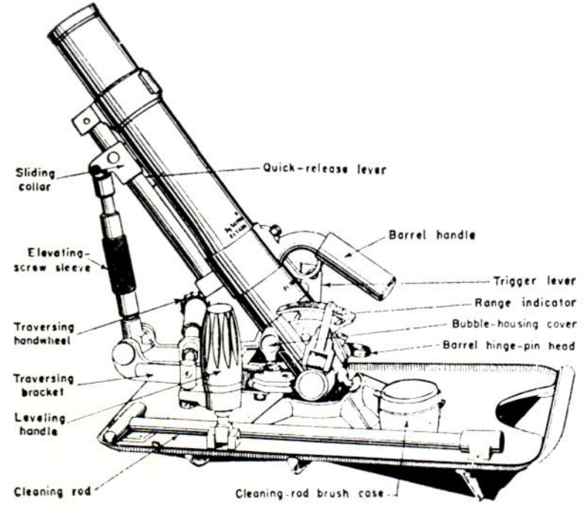

LEFT: Standard light mortar was the 5 cm l.gr.W. 36. It was trigger-fired and had a crew of three and maximum range of 568 yards. It broke into two parts (barrel and baseplate) for carrying. Weight was 31 pounds (US Official).

Appendix 1: Heer (Army) and Waffen-SS ranks and their equivalents

Army (Heer)	Waffen-SS	British	U.S.
Schütze (1)	Schütze	Private	Private
Oberschütze (2)	Oberschütze	Private (senior)	PFC
Gefreiter	Sturmmann	Lance Corporal	Acting Corporal
Obergefreiter	Rottenführer	Corporal	Corporal
Unteroffizier	Uterscharführer	Lance Sergeant	Sergeant
Unterfeldwebel	Scharführer	Sergeant	Staff Sergeant
Feldwebel	Oberscharführer	Company Sergeant Major	Technical Sergeant
Oberfeldwebel	Hauptscharführer	Sergeant Major	Master Sergeant
Hauptfeldwebel	Stabsscharführer	RSM	First Sergeant
Stabsfeldwebel	Sturmscharführer	Staff Sergeant	Master Sergeant
Leutnant	Untersturmführer	2nd Lieutenant	2nd Lieutenant
Oberleutnant	Obersturmführer	Lieutenant	1st Lieutenant
Hauptmann	Hauptsturmführer	Captain	Captain
Major	Sturmbannführer	Major	Major
Obertstleutnant	Obersturmbannführer	Lieutenant Colonel	Lieutenant Colonel
Oberst	Standartenführer	Colonel	Colonel
—	Oberführer	Brigadier	Brigadier-General
		Major General	Brigadier-General
Generalmajor	Brigadeführer	Lieutenant General	Major General
Generalleutnant	Gruppenführer	General	Lieutenant-General
General der Infantrie (3)	Obergruppenführer	General	General
Generaloberst	Oberstgruppenführer	Field Marshal	General of Army
Generalfeldmarschall	Reichführer der SS	No equivalent	No equivalent

NOTES

(1) Term for 'Riflemen'. From late 1942 all riflemen became Grenadiers. In other arms the equivalent was 'Pioneer' (Engineers), 'Reiter' (Cavalry), 'Jager' (Light Infantry/Mountain Troops), Kanonier (Artillery).

(2) Or 'Obergrenadier,' etc.

(3) Or 'General der Artillerie,' 'General der Kavallerie,' 'General der Panzertruppe,' etc.

Appendix 2: Infantry Regiment, 1942

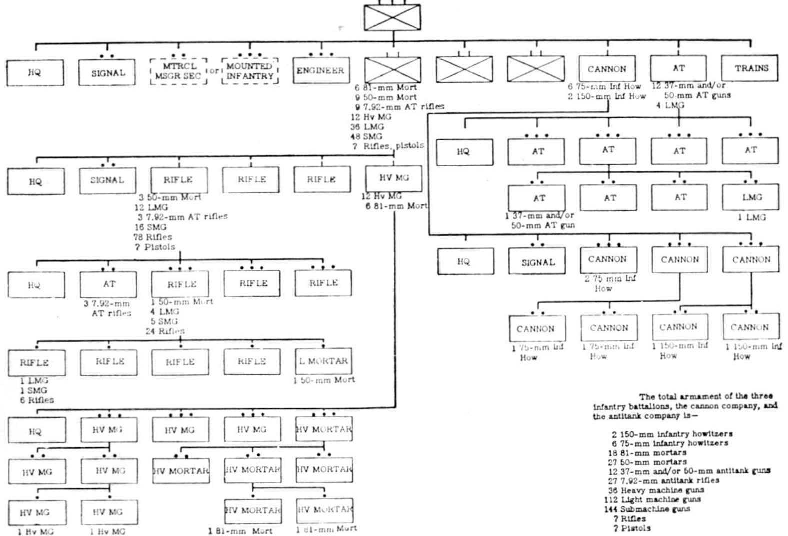

This table shows the organisation of a typical three battalion infantry regiment and gives an indication of the firepower available.

Appendix 3: For further study

THIS book is intended to give a broad basic coverage of German combat uniforms in World War 2. Several books in the Almark range deal with individual subjects in much greater detai and contain further information and more illustrations. These are listed below:

Gebirgsjäger (Wehrmacht Illustrated series)
Africa Korps (Wehrmacht Illustrated series)
Panzer-Grenadiers (Wehrmacht Illustrated series)
Waffen-SS, by D. S. V. Fosten and R. J. Marrion
***Fallschirmjager**, by J. Lucas and R. C. Gibson
***Luftwaffe: Uniforms and Insignia**, by M. Cooper and J. Lucas
***Flags and Banners of the Third Reich**, by A. S. Walker and F. Stephens
(* published in 1973)

THE following large reference books deal with aspects of German military uniforms in encyclopaedic detail and are commended for a really extensive study of the subject.

German Army Uniforms and Insignia, 1933-1945, by B. L. Davis (Arms & Armour)
Uniforms of the SS, Vols 1-7, by A. Moll (Historical Research Unit)